# JAGENDORF'S
# FOUNDRY

# JAGENDORF'S FOUNDRY

## Memoir of the Romanian Holocaust 1941–1944

*Siegfried Jagendorf*

*Introduction and Commentaries by*
ARON HIRT-MANHEIMER

■ HarperCollins*Publishers*

Jagendorf's Foundry: Memoir of the Romanian Holocaust 1941–1944.

Copyright © 1991 by Ralph D. Stern and Dr. Edith Gitman.

FIRST EDITION

Designed by Irving Perkins Associates

---

Library of Congress Cataloging-in-Publication Data

Jagendorf, Siegfried, 1885–1970.
  Jagendorf's foundry : memoir of the Romanian Holocaust, 1941–1944 / by Siegfried Jagendorf ; introduction and commentaries by Aron Hirt-Manheimer.—1st ed.
    p.  cm.
  Includes bibliographical references (p.   ) and index.
  ISBN 0-06-016106-X
  1. Jews—Romania—Persecutions.  2. Holocaust, Jewish (1939–1945)—Romania—Personal narratives.  3. Jagendorf, Siegfried, 1885–1970.
  4. World War, 1939–1945—Jews—Rescue—Ukraine—Transnistria.
  5. Romania—Ethnic relations.  6. Transnistria—Ethnic relations.
  I. Hirt-Manheimer, Aron, 1948–  II. Title.
DS135.R7J3  1991
940.53'18–dc20                                                      90-55540

---

91  92  93  94  95  AC/RRD  10  9  8  7  6  5  4  3  2  1

*In memory of the martyrs of Transnistria—
the "Forgotten Cemetery"*

# CONTENTS

*Part Three*
# SPRING–SUMMER, 1942

*Part Four*
# FALL, 1942

*Part Five*
# WINTER, 1942–1943

*Part Six*
# SPRING–SUMMER, 1943

*Part Seven*
# 1944–1946

# INTRODUCTION

$A$UTUMN, 1941. Romania exiles an estimated 150,000 Jews to a war-devastated corner of the occupied Soviet Ukraine. Max Schmidt remembers:

"We reached a God–forsaken border town called Atachi, a landscape of endless mud. Romanian soldiers chased us from the cattle train. 'Faster, faster,' they yelled, beating us with clubs, seizing our baggage. After an excruciating blow to my hand, I dropped the valise containing my academic certificates. A soldier scooped up the prize. At dusk we were forced into a grotto-like shelter, the ground swarming with people. In the blackness a woman gave birth.

"Our tormentors roused us in the morning with whips and clubs. They were heartless, inhuman. One tore off a woman's golden earring, the flesh still attached. My wife and I merged with the frightful mass streaming toward the Dniester River. I slid from the path and sank to the shoulders into a pit of mud. My wife reached toward me, but the stampede swept her away. I had lost all hope, when a strong hand reached down and dredged me out. The mass took him before I could offer thanks.

"That night, a primitive barge ferried us across the Dniester. We regrouped in Moghilev–Podolski, a city deluged by fire and flood. A man told me that a deportee from Radauti—Engineer Siegfried Jagendorf—was organizing professionals for work. I set out at once to find him. On the streets Ukrainian thugs and Romanian soldiers preyed on the exiles. How strange, I thought, to hear Ukrainians speaking one language, Romanians another, but understanding each other perfectly on the subject of Jews.

"I located the Radauti people in a large building near the river and approached a woman standing in the courtyard. Introducing myself as Engineer Max Schmidt from Cernauti, I inquired about Engineer Jagendorf. She told me he was meeting with the prefect and would return shortly. I asked how I would recognize him. 'By his white collar,' she answered."

Max Schmidt had no difficulty distinguishing Siegfried Jagendorf from the other Jewish deportees. The 56-year-old former Siemens executive displayed not the slightest sign of having just stepped from a death train. His suit was clean, shoes polished. He wore kid gloves and puffed a cigarette from an eight-inch holder. While other Jews were scrambling for a crust of bread or a place to hide, Siegfried Jagendorf secured an audience with the Romanian prefect and emerged holding the key to Jewish survival.

Jagendorf took control of the Jewish ghetto and established a soup kitchen, hospitals, and orphanages. His hand-picked team of Jewish professionals and craftsmen restored a sabotaged foundry and spare-parts factory that became the nucleus of an effort that would save as many as 10,000 lives. The achievement was termed "the miracle of Moghilev" by Matatias Carp, chronicler of Romania's genocidal assault upon its Jewish minority.

The central figure of this miracle, Siegfried Jagendorf, enjoyed a privileged position amid the naked squalor of Moghilev. He ruled the enslaved colony with an iron hand. Two bodyguards prevented Jews from approaching him. A receptionist sat before the soundproof door of his office, warding off petitioners. Romanian officials shook his hand. Soldiers clicked their heels and saluted the Jewish "kaiser."

Siegfried Jagendorf and his wife, Hilda, survived the war and in December, 1946, were reunited with their two daughters and grandchildren in the United States. At age 61, Jagendorf was weary and penniless but determined to regain his professional stature. Four years later, he secured a job at the Los Angeles offices of a large electrical contracting firm. In 1956, he began writing this memoir in his adopted language but failed to find a publisher. Jagendorf fell terminally ill in 1970 at the age of 85 and died without seeing his story in print. In 1973, his widow sent a copy of the unpublished memoir and the Moghilev files to the Yad Vashem Holocaust Martyrs' and Heroes' Remembrance Authority in Jerusalem, which established an archive in Jagendorf's name.

Fifteen years later, Lawrence J. Gitman brought a copy of his grandfather's manuscript to an associate publisher at Harper-Collins. She promptly signed a contract with Jagendorf's heirs and asked me to substantiate the story, provide background information, and polish the prose. I spent the next two years analyzing translations of hundreds of Romanian and German documents and interviewing Jagendorf family members and Moghilev survivors. My findings form the basis of the book's commentaries, which fill in gaps and provide various perspectives and divergent interpretations that sometimes reinforce and sometimes refute the author's account.

Jagendorf portrayed himself as a stern but sympathetic leader who saved his people by outmaneuvering Romanian officials and by converting a bewildered mob into a productive labor force. This self-portrayal posed a dilemma. In order to survive, Jewish workers served the interests of Romanian and German mass murderers. Was this passive resistance or collaboration with the enemy, or both? More specifically, did Jagendorf collaborate with the Romanians in oppressing his own people, or did he induce Romanian officials to collaborate with him in redeeming the victims? The commentaries raise questions about Jagendorf's motives and moral character. Was he an opportunist who usurped power to preserve his own life, or a selfless humanitarian who placed the welfare of others before his own? Did he rule with an iron fist because he relished power, or because he knew no other way to govern a desperate people in a lawless land?

---

Schmiel Jagendorf was born on August 1, 1885, in the northern Bukovina village of Zviniace. The youngest of four children and the only son, Schmiel was doted on by his parents, Abraham Jagendorf and Hannah Bassie Offenberger. Typical of Orthodox Jews in this region of the Austro-Hungarian Empire,

Schmiel's bearded father wore a black caftan and skullcap; his mother concealed her hair under an embroidered kerchief. Schmiel and his sisters—Bertha, Betti, and Mina—spent their youth on the family farm, living in simple comfort alongside a river that powered the wheel of the flour mill owned and operated by their father. The Jagendorfs also owned a small herd of livestock.

Like the other Jewish boys of his village, Schmiel received a traditional religious education. As an adolescent, however, he began to reject the tethered lifestyle of the Orthodox and the limited vistas of the village. The miller's son dreamed of studying in Vienna or Berlin. After completing the first four years of gymnasium (secondary school), he enrolled in a three-year mechanical engineering program at the Technical Trade-Museum in Vienna, apprenticing in its workshops. While a student in Vienna, Jagendorf joined a student Zionist organization. According to family lore, he received the honor of being a pall-bearer at Theodor Herzl's funeral in 1904.

Jagendorf had a scar across his forehead, which his descendants attribute to a duel he fought with a Jew-baiter at the University of Heidelberg. School records show, however, that "Sami" Jagendorf studied at the Technikum Mittweida, a well-respected German technical school near Dresden. He majored in general engineering, specializing in toolmaking. Jagendorf scored high marks, excelling in German language studies. He also demonstrated a talent for shortcutting the system: skipping classes, avoiding difficult exams and receiving the diploma in advance of his classmates. On November 17, 1905, a Mittweida physician, Dr. Moebias, informed the school that Sami Jagendorf was suffering from a heart condition. In consideration of his sudden malady, Jagendorf gained the school's forgiveness for his frequent absences and overdue assignments, and a full exemption from the drafting table.

Jagendorf completed the three-year program at Mittweida six months early, receiving his diploma in electrical and mechanical engineering on May 31, 1907. The Mittweida degree certified Jagendorf's use of the title "electro-technician."

Sami Jagendorf married Hinde Feller in the Bukovina town

of Radautz (Rădăuţi in Romanian) on May 9, 1909. Before the wedding, the robust, six-foot-tall groom with fair hair and blue eyes adopted the valorous German name "Siegfried." His graceful 21-year-old bride, the second daughter of David and Zissel Feller, proprietors of a pickled herring concern in Radautz, became "Hilda."

Not the slightest vestige of the religious rural life could be detected in the appearance or manner of the dapper Jagendorf, who sported a handlebar moustache, top hat, cane, and elongated cigarette holder that would become his trademark. On rare visits to his birthplace, Siegfried would seat Hilda in the sidecar of his motorcycle and speed through the countryside, hurling clouds of dust and smoke into the sky. Terrified peasants fell trembling to their knees before the thundering contraption, much to the amusement of the young couple.

Hilda gave birth to two daughters, Elfreda and Edith. The girls were reared in the cultural traditions of Austro-Hungarian Empire. Siegfried and Hilda regarded Vienna as their Jerusalem and German as their sacred tongue. Siegfried showed no tolerance for the religious way of life, denying his daughters a Jewish education, even forbidding them to fast on Yom Kippur, the day of atonement. Membership in a charitable B'nai B'rith lodge constituted Jagendorf's only Jewish institutional involvement.

Jagendorf's service as a first lieutenant in the Austrian army during World War I earned him the Franz Joseph medal, the empire's highest military decoration. He had supervised the construction of an electrified security fence along a stretch of the Bukovina–Russian border. When the Russians breached the barrier, they came looking for Jagendorf and put a bounty on his head. Hilda and the girls fled Czernowitz (Cernăuţi in Romanian, Chernovtsy in Russian) to the Transylvanian town of Bistrita-Nasaud, where they remained for two months before joining Siegfried in Vienna.

After the war, Jagendorf found employment with Siemens–Schukert Werke in Vienna, where he took advantage of a law passed in 1917 authorizing the city's Ministry of Public Works to confer professional titles upon individuals with proven ability.

The Mittweida graduate could now call himself Engineer Jagendorf. When, in February, 1922, Siemens–Schukert appointed Jagendorf director of its Bukovina sales and service operations, he moved his family to Cernauti, the Bukovina capital, and opted for Romanian citizenship. They owned and lived in a spacious apartment building at Neue Weltgasse 10, which also housed the Siemens–Schukert showroom and offices. The well-paid executive rented a villa on the outskirts of Cernauti and later bought a home on the grounds of a castle in the heart of Vienna.

The Jagendorfs lived in high style. They were served by a large staff of domestic retainers, wore only hand-tailored clothes from Europe's fashion capitals, gave lavish dinner parties on tables set to perfection with the finest silver and china. They took summer vacations at resort spas in Carlsbad and Vatra Dornei, traveled to the French Riviera in their chaffeured Italian motor car, and attended galas at the homes of the Jewish aristocracy in Budapest.

Daughters Elfreda and Edith attended finishing school in Switzerland and received instruction at home from their French governess. At parties, where their father loved to surround himself with admirers, the girls were displayed like porcelain dolls in their petticoated dresses and matching hair bows.

Jagendorf placed tremendous emphasis on clothes and personal grooming. "He was the neatest of men," according to Elfreda, "just like his father in the caftan, who always looked spotless. Father's clothes were custom tailored, his shoes always polished, his jacket brushed, fingernails manicured. He was definitely the continental type, sitting with his legs crossed, smoking a cigarette in a long holder, charming you with his broad smile and deep laugh. He walked erect and looked you straight in the eye. I always admired the striking beauty of his hands."

Working for a time as her father's secretary, Elfreda observed that he had a "fabulous memory for details, an attorney's understanding of contracts, and a gift for composing business letters. Before making an important decision, he would sit for days at his desk, smoking cigarettes and gazing into the air.

Then he would act decisively. He had the power of persuasion and knew how to sell his ideas. He demanded and received deference, always finding his way to the top. He knew how to delegate responsibility. Left alone, he couldn't even install an electrical fixture."

Elfreda and Edith point out that their father insisted on absolute obedience in his household, reproving family and staff for the slightest lapse. The girls could speak only when addressed. His inflexibility and frequent tirades created a tense and oppressive atmosphere. Only Elfreda dared to defy the master of the house, who would react by not speaking to her for weeks. Elfreda recalls that, on one occasion, he threatened her with a horse whip after she refused to go to school in an uncomfortable dress. "My sister Edith suffered a severe case of frostbite because he insisted that we wear ankle socks in subzero temperature." Elfreda says she received little support from their mother, who adored her husband and "yes'd him all the time." The daughters concur that Siegfried Jagendorf often treated his wife with disdain, dismissing her opinions with the comment, *"Was weisst Du?"* (What do you know?). In fact, Elfreda found her father to be intolerant of any woman who expressed an independent viewpoint.

Edith recalls only one time when her father showed her warmth and affection: "Just before beginning my medical studies, I got cold feet. My father sat down at the side of the bed and said, 'Why don't you go, and if you don't like it, you can back out.' That was the only fatherly thing he ever did. It was just what I needed at that time."

Jagendorf resigned from Siemens–Schukert in 1923, after one year in his Bukovina post. The company agreed to pay him the then-considerable sum of 500,000 lei ($5,000), "to satisfy your pretentions . . . against this enterprise and furthermore as an indemnity." (Because Siemens maintained no records from that period, it is impossible to ascertain the nature of the dispute.) For the next four years, Jagendorf served as general director of Foresta, the society of the lumber industry in Bukovina. Having amassed the equivalent of a half-million dollars by that time, Jagendorf went into business for himself, with disastrous results. The charcoal briquette factory he built in Vienna, Licalit, was destroyed by fire, and his radio manufacturing enterprise in Cernauti failed as a result of embezzlement by a top manager.

In March, 1938, when German forces entered Austria, Jagendorf found himself trapped in Vienna, where he was attempting to revive his briquette business. A friend who had joined the Austrian Nazi Party offered to accompany Jagendorf to the train station, heavily guarded by police and Gestapo agents. He handed Jagendorf a swastika lapel pin to aid his escape. After a two-day journey through Czechoslovakia and the southern tip of Poland, Jagendorf arrived at the Romanian border. Citing a visa violation, the police chief refused to permit the pauperized engineer into the country and threatened to deport him back to Vienna. Jagendorf contacted family members in Radauti, who raised the bribe necessary for his release.

Edith and her husband, William Gitman, an American studying medicine in Switzerland, fled Europe in 1938. Elfreda and her husband, Henry Stern, an opthalmologist, emigrated to the United States from Austria the following year. Escaping Romania proved more difficult for Siegfried and Hilda, who for the next three years sought without success to reach America. On October 12, 1941, they and most of the other Jews of Radauti were loaded aboard a cattle train and deported across Romania's northern frontier to the southwest region of the Soviet Ukraine, recently vanquished by German and Romanian armies.

---

Bucharest's decision to banish the Jews of its northern provinces to Transnistria, (from the Romanian "trans-Nistru"), the land across the Dniester River, culminated more than a decade of virulent anti-Semitic agitation in a nation historically hostile toward its Jewish minority. In 1923 Romania was the last European nation to grant Jews citizenship, and did so only under duress. The target of perpetual Easter pogroms, the *Evrei* (Hebrews) played the traditional role of scapegoat for superstitious Christian peasants. Jews were blamed and punished for the calamities endured by a nation that had been impoverished and debased by a succession of cruel conquerors and corrupt leaders. The Romanian learned to curse the Turk, the Russian, the Hungarian . . . and to beat the Jew.

Romania's fortunes improved following World War I, when the victorious Allied powers awarded her three long-disputed territories: Bessarabia from Russia, Bukovina from Austria, and Transylvania from Hungary. Acquisition of these provinces added more than a half million unwanted Jews to Greater Romania. The insistence of the Allies at the Versailles peace talks that Romania honor its obligation to grant Jews full citizenship and civil rights unleashed a violent xenophobic backlash, particularly among anti-Semitic university students and intellectuals who rallied the nation around the slogan: "Romania for the Romanians." It was during this period that Corneliu Codreanu founded the Legion of the Archangel Michael. His legionary movement, also known as the Iron Guard, glorified the unspoiled peasant farmer as the purest incarnation of God and country and regarded assassination and martyrdom as the most noble path to purifying the nation of corruption (politicians) and of evil on earth (Jews).

In the 1920s, the Jews of Romania benefited from the constitutional reforms that allowed them full civil rights; however, the great depression of 1929 devastated the nation's largely agricultural economy and undermined Iuliu Maniu's ruling National Peasant Party. Romania's fledgling democracy began its decline in June, 1930, when King Carol II returned from exile and reclaimed the crown from his eight-year-old son Michael. Carol had been forced to abdicate after choosing his half-Jewish mistress, Madame Lupescu, over his wife, Queen Helena. Prime Minister Iuliu Maniu permitted the king's return on condition that his "royal concubine" remain behind. King Carol betrayed his promise, arriving in Bucharest with the "serpent seductress" at his side. The elected leader resigned in protest, allowing King Carol to fill the power vacuum by establishing a royal dictatorship.

In the 1930s, Hitler's rise to power in Germany bolstered Romania's anti-Semitic legions. Three days after Christmas, 1937, King Carol installed the nation's first avowedly anti-

Semitic government. Led by the nationally renowned poet Octavian Goga and the veteran Jew-baiter A. C. Cuza, the regime moved quickly to strip more than half the nation's Jews of their citizenship. The government seized Jewish businesses and deprived the *jidani* (kikes) of jobs and education. The regime lasted little more than a month but set the pattern that, in the next five years, would virtually destroy the third largest Jewish population in Europe.

In February, 1938, the Romanian monarch suspended the nation's constitution and outlawed all opposition parties. He began to abandon Romania's traditional alliance with France and Great Britain in favor of the more powerful Germany. King Carol traveled to Berlin to sign economic accords granting Hitler full access to Romania's natural resources at bargain prices, including vast petroleum reserves that in summer, 1941, would help fuel the Nazi invasion of the Soviet Union.

Romania's economic concessions did not prevent Berlin from betraying Bucharest. In August, 1939, Hitler and Stalin concluded a pact that contained a secret provision returning Bessarabia to Soviet sovereignty. Ten months later, the Soviet foreign minister, Vyacheslav M. Molotov, issued an ultimatum demanding the evacuation within 48 hours of all Romanian forces from Bessarabia, the territory that Romania took from the Russians after World War I. As penalty payment, the Soviets also helped themselves to northern Bukovina. Rich in lumber, cattle, grain, and minerals, these territories accounted for a large share of Romania's export income.

On Germany's cynical advice, Romania retreated without firing a shot, except at Jews, who were blamed for the humiliating defeat. Romanian Jewish soldiers were killed by being pushed from moving trains. Pogroms erupted in the districts of Dorohoi, Storojinet, and Suceava.

King Carol reorganized his cabinet on July 4, 1940, and selected a pro-Nazi gold mine owner, Ion Gigurtu, to head the government. The king declared an amnesty for members of the outlawed Iron Guard, and its commander, Horia Sima (founder Corneliu Codreanu had been murdered by order of King Carol), returned from exile in Germany to serve in the new government as minister of education and enlightenment. The Gigurtu regime wasted no time in enacting even harsher anti-Semitic legislation. These included dismissal of Jews from the army and civil service, from editorial posts and corporate board rooms; the imposition of restrictions in the practice of law and other professions; and prohibitions regarding the purchase of properties and businesses. More ominous, the definition of "Jew" was based on the German Nuremberg Laws that categorized Jews as belonging to a race rather than to a religion. Thus, a Jew could not escape persecution by converting to Christianity.

Ion Gigurtu resigned in August, 1940, after the Germans engineered an even more painful territorial amputation from the body of Greater Romania. Bucharest was forced to cede the northern half of Transylvania to Hungary, an enemy of Romania but an ally of Germany. Again, the Romanian army offered no resistance. Thousands of Romanians wept in the streets during three days of national mourning; mobs threw stones at the palace, cursing the king, the Germans . . . and the Jews.

The dishonored monarch called upon General Ion Antonescu, the former defense minister of the Goga–Cuza regime, to form a new cabinet. On September 6, 1940, General Antonescu demanded that King Carol abdicate in favor of his eighteen-year-old son Michael. After obtaining Antonescu's permission to flee to Spain, the deposed king and his mistress stocked a nine-carriage train with a fleet of bullet-proof automobiles, $2,500,000 worth of Madame Lupescu's jewelry, and a cache of gold. A contingent of Iron Guard assassins waited in ambush at Timisoara, but the train did not stop to take on water as planned. The guardists opened fire, sending Carol and his mistress diving for cover into the royal bathtub as the abdication train raced across the border to safety. Antonescu then went on radio and called upon the people to go to church and "blaspheme" the disgraced king and his supporters for dishonoring the nation.

The diminutive Antonescu, nicknamed "Red Dog" for his coloring and mercurial personality, declared himself *Conducator*—the Romanian equivalent of *Führer*. Although he had not been a member of the Iron Guard, Antonescu donned a green shirt and proclaimed the "National Legionary State" on September 14, 1940. He appointed a cabinet of generals and legionnaires, headed by law professor Mihai Antonescu (no relation). The commander of the Iron Guard, Horia Sima, became vice premier, and other prominent legionary leaders occupied key cabinet posts.

Antonescu's alliance with the Iron Guard disintegrated several months later, when the legionnaires refused to end their homicidal excesses. On January 21, 1941, Horia Sima, confident of Berlin's backing, attempted to overthrow Antonescu, but Hitler favored the general, telling him: "I don't need fanatics, I need a healthy Romanian army." Without German support, the revolt degenerated into a pogrom with Bucharest at its center. American journalist Robert St. John witnessed the Iron Guard in action, as reported in his book, *Foreign Correspondent:*

"Accounts of the atrocities committed by the legionnaires during the thirty-six hour pogram might never have been believed by anyone, except that we saw some of it happen, we counted the corpses, we noted the mutilations, we inspected what little was left of the seven once-beautiful synagogues, we saw the whole quarter in ruins, and we took careful notes. . . .

"During the night, members of the Legion of the Archangel Michael . . . went to the homes of some of Bucharest's most distinguished Jews and loaded nearly two hundred men and women into trucks. The victims were taken to the abattoir on the edge of the city. There they were stripped naked, forced to get down on all fours, and were driven up the ramp of the slaughterhouse. Then they were put through all the stages of animals at slaughter until finally the beheaded bodies, spurting blood, were hung on iron hooks along the wall. As a last sadistic touch the legionnaires took rubber stamps and branded the carcasses with the Romanian equivalent of: FIT FOR HUMAN CONSUMPTION." St. John sums up his impression of the Romanians: "volatile, unpredictable, corrupt beyond imagination, and cruel beyond forgiveness."

The Iron Guard continued its wild rampage of slaughter and

plunder for three days and three nights before Antonescu finally ordered the army to crush the rebellion. The Nazis spirited Horia Sima and 300 of his legionnaires out of the country and billeted them in comfortable quarters on the fringes of several German concentration camps, where the SS kept them on hand for possible intervention against Antonescu.

Having subdued the Iron Guard, General Antonescu restructured his cabinet in February, 1941, appointing Goga–Cuzists and military officers. If Romania's Jews thought the change might improve their safety, an event in the Moldavian city of Iasi (Jassy) proved otherwise. As the Romanian and German armies invaded the Soviet Union on June 22, 1941, a rumor circulated that Jews had sheltered Soviet spies and shot at Romanian soldiers. The unsubstantiated allegations served as a pretext for Marshal Antonescu, as he now called himself, to order the execution of fifty Jews for every soldier killed. In the pogrom that followed, more than 10,000 Jewish civilians lost their lives. The Italian war correspondent Curzio Malaparte wrote an eye-witness account of the terror in his book, *Kaputt*:

"Hordes of Jews pursued by soldiers and maddened civilians armed with knives and crowbars fled along the streets; groups of policemen smashed in house doors with their rifle butts; windows opened suddenly and screaming disheveled women in nightgowns appeared with their arms raised in the air; some threw themselves from windows and their faces hit the asphalt with a dull thud. Squads of soldiers hurled hand grenades . . . into the cellars where many people had vainly sought safety. . . . Where the slaughter had been heaviest, the feet slipped in blood; everywhere the hysterical and ferocious toll of the pogrom filled the houses and streets with shots, with weeping, with terrible screams and with cruel laughter."

Jews who escaped the initial onslaught were rounded up and executed in the courtyard of the police station or packed into sealed trains that rolled through the countryside with no purpose other than to exterminate its human freight. The trains stopped periodically to eject bodies, again described by Malaparte:

"The soldiers climbed into the car and began throwing out

the corpses one by one. There were a hundred and seventy-nine of them—all suffocated, all had swollen heads and bluish faces. Meanwhile, a squad of German soldiers and a little crowd of local inhabitants and peasants had come up and helped open the cars, throw out the corpses, and range them along the railway embankment. . . . A crowd of peasants and gypsies who had gathered from all over were stripping the corpses. . . . The dead seemed to defend themselves with all their strength against the violence of those who were stripping them; men and women dripping with perspiration, screaming and cursing, were doggedly trying to raise stubborn arms, bend stiff elbows and knees, in order to draw off the jackets, trousers and underclothing. The women were most stubborn in their relentless defense. I never thought that it would be so difficult to take a slip off a dead girl. Perhaps it was modesty still alive in them that gave the women the strength to defend themselves; sometimes they raised themselves on their elbows, brought their white faces near to the sweaty faces of those who profaned them. . . ."

The Nazis disparaged the pogrom as a barbaric display. Malaparte recounts a conversation with Hans Frank, the governor-general of occupied Poland, and two other high-ranking Nazi officials:

" 'How many Jews were killed in Jassy that night;' Frank asked me in an ironical voice as he stretched out his feet toward the fire and laughed softly". . . .

" 'The official report issued by the vice-president of the Council, Mihai Antonescu," I replied, "admitted that there were five hundred. But the official count by Colonel Lupu was seven thousand slaughtered Jews.'

" 'Quite a respectable figure,' said Frank, 'but it was not a decent way to do it; it is not necessary to do it that way. . . . The Romanians are not a civilized people. . . .'

" 'Pogroms are a Slavic specialty," said Wachter (governor of Cracow). 'In all things, we Germans are guided by reason and method and not by bestial instincts; we always act scientifically. . . . We use surgeons not butchers. . . .' "

Less than a week after the Iasi pogrom, a grim foreshadowing of Romanian's solution to the Jewish question in Bukovina and Bessarabia, Mihai Antonescu, president of the council of ministers, told administration officials what fate his government had ordained for the Jews of these provinces:

"We are now at the moment in time most favorable for ethnic liberation, national revision and the purification of our nation from all those elements alien to her soul, which have grown like weeds, darkening her future. In order that this unique moment not be lost, we must be implacable. . . ."

A few days later, Marshal Ion Antonescu clarified the policy to the cabinet:

"I am for the forced migration of the entire Jewish element from Bessarabia and Bukovina, which must be thrown over the [Russian] border. . . . You must be merciless . . . I do not know when . . . the Romanian nation will again enjoy this total freedom of action, with the possibility for ethnic purification and national revision. This is the hour when we are masters on our territory. Let it be used! I do not mind if history judges us barbarians. . . . If need be, shoot with machine guns, and I say that there is no law. . . ."

After a month of fighting, Axis forces recovered the "lost provinces" of Bessarabia and northern Bukovina, which the Soviets had seized the previous summer in accordance with the secret Hitler–Stalin Pact. Aided by the gendarmerie, the Romanian Third Army and security forces carried out unwritten "special orders" to "cleanse the ground" of Jews. As Dr. Jean Ancel of Yad Vashem has observed: "The crimes were not committed by Romanian individual accomplices but by the entire state apparatus: the Romanian army, gendarmerie, police, civil authorities, prefectures, city councils and tribunals." Premeditated and uncoerced, the Romanian regime presided over the extermination of tens of thousands of Jewish civilians—old and young, women and men—in retaliation for illusory offenses. It was the recurring blood libel on a colossal scale. Instead of falsely accusing a single Jew of ritual murder, thousands of Jews were unjustly indicted for shedding the blood of Romanian soldiers.

The Jews of Bessarabia received the most brutal treatment

and suffered the heaviest losses; of an estimated 207,000 at the time of the Axis invasion, only about 20,000 remained. On July 17, 1941 German and Romanian troops stormed into the Bessarabian city of Chisinau (Kishinev) and slaughtered more than ten thousand Jews. Similar atrocities wiped out the rural Jewish populations in the first days of the occupation. The Romanians then established ghettos and concentration camps in preparation for mass deportations of Jews across the Dniester River.

In fall, 1941, the Romanian government deported 140,000–150,000 Jews from Bessarabia, Bukovina, and Dorohoi to a region in the western Ukraine approximately twice the size of New Jersey. The territory, conquered by Romanian and German forces in the first weeks of Operation Barbarossa (code name for the secret invasion of Soviet Union) was designated "Transnistria" and awarded by Hitler to Antonescu in recognition of Romania's contributions to the war effort. An artificial geographical entity that existed from 1941 to 1944, Transnistria was bordered on the west by the Dniester River, on the east by the Bug River, on the south by the Black Sea, and on the north by a line beyond Moghilev.

Here the exiled Jews were expected to perish of "natural causes," nameless victims of a world at war; accordingly, the Romanian administration denied the deportees food, water, soap, clothes, fuel, shelter, and medicine. Forced on death marches to remote localities throughout the approximately 16,000-square mile territory, thousands died of exhaustion, disease, and exposure. Those who fell behind were beaten or shot. Naked, decomposing corpses on the roadside became the leitmotif of the Romanian government's crusade to exploit a "historical opportunity" to rid the nation of its unwanted Jewish minority.

With rare exception, Romania's political, intellectual, and ecclesiastical leaders did not speak out against the deportations to Transnistria. Almost all interventions were initiated by Jews, most significantly those of the young chief rabbi, Alexandre Safran, and of Dr. Wilhelm Filderman, the communal president of Romanian Jewry.

In a passionate letter to the dictator, dated October 11, 1941,

Dr. Filderman implored Marshal Antonescu to renounce the deportations from the Chisinau ghetto in Bessarabia:

"I have today received a desperate appeal from the head of the Ghetto of Chisinau. . . . On the morning of the 8th of October of this year, 1,500 people were taken away, the majority on foot, bringing with them only what they could carry. Thus almost all of them [are] badly dressed and exposed to the cold, without food and denied the possibility of supplying themselves for a journey of at least eight days in rain, frost and snow. . . . This is death, death, death of innocent people with no other guilt than that of being Jews. I implore you again, Mr. Marshal, not to permit such a staggering tragedy to take place."

Marshal Antonescu released his reply to the press on October 27th, three days after his army massacred more than 40,000 Jewish civilians in the Ukrainian port city of Odessa. Denying that Jews were without guilt, the military dictator wrote:

"Did you give any thought last year to what was in our hearts during the evacuation of Bessarabia, and to what is happening to us daily and hourly when we are paying dearly with our blood . . . for the hatred of your coreligionists in Bessarabia?

"What did you do last year when you heard how the Jews of Bessarabia and Bukovina behaved toward the withdrawing Romanian troops who until then had defended the peace and wealth of those Jews? I will remind you:

"Even before the appearance of the Soviet troops, the Jews of Bessarabia and Bukovina, whom you are defending, spat upon our officers, tore off their epaulets, ripped their uniforms, and, when they could, beat and killed our soldiers like cowards. We have proof.

"Those same wretches greeted the arrival of Soviet troops with flowers and celebrated with great joy. We have photographs to prove that. . . .

"From the cellars in Chisinau our martyrs are removed daily, terribly mutilated cadavers thus rewarded for the friendly hand which, for twenty years, they stretched out to those ungrateful beasts. . . .

"Do not pity, if you really have a soul, those who do not merit it; pity those who merit it.

"Cry with those mothers, who cried in agony over their lost children, not with those who have done themselves and are doing you so much harm."

Filderman responded on October 25, professing personal and communal Jewish loyalty to Romania and arguing that "the guilty should be punished without pity, but that tens of thousands of innocent people cannot be punished for the deeds of the guilty. . . . Neither can all the Jews of Romania be held responsible for the deeds of the Jews of Russia."

Disassociating the Romanian Jewish leadership from Bolshevism, Filderman wrote: "Conscientious Jews throughout the world have disavowed Communism and Communist Jews, as have the rabbis of Romania. . . ."

Pleading for a postponement of the deportations, Filderman offered "the best proof" of the Jews' unwavering loyalty to Romania: ". . . Since your assumption of leadership of the state, not a single Jew throughout Romania has been found working against the regime. Since the beginning of the war, the Jewish population has demonstrated its loyalty to the German army and to our army; above all, the day following mobilization, I made a plea in writing for the reinstatement of the Jews in the army to permit them, like their forefathers in the War of Independence, in the Balkan War, and the War of Restoration, to give their lives side by side with the Romanian soldier for the triumph of the Romanian cause, for a great and powerful Romania."

Antonescu ignored Filderman's patriotic appeal, holding to his unsubstantiated contention that the Jews of Bukovina and Bessarabia uniformly favored Bolshevism and therefore deserved communal exile. He extended the accusation as well to the Jews of southern Bukovina and Dorohoi, areas that never had come under Soviet rule. Had Antonescu wanted to give Filderman a truthful reply, he would have repeated a remark quoted by a Spanish diplomat to the American envoy: "This is wartime, a good time to settle the Jewish problem once and for all."

Chief Rabbi Alexandre Safran recalls Antonescu's reaction to his plea for compassion and mercy:

"When I finally met him, emotion filled my words, my tone, my insistence. I begged him to take pity on those wretched, dislocated, hunted people and not to send them to their deaths. At a certain moment it seemed that he was touched, but soon he started to rant and rave. I tried to calm him, to point out that, with but one word, he could stop the catastrophe. . . . But he merely stared at me severely with his sometimes burning, some-times icy eyes, and maintained that the Jews deserved their fate. His face grew alternately bright red and pale white, and he appeared like a wild beast ready to tear me to shreds. . . . I already started murmuring *Shema Israel* (Hear O Israel—an affirmation of faith chanted by Jews in worship and in the most dire of circumstances)."

The U.S. representative in Bucharest, Franklin Mott Gunther, wired Washington in early November, 1941, after three months of deportations:

". . .Only a relatively small number of Jews are believed now to be left in Bessarabia . . . while in Bukovina there are, accord-ing to reliable Jews, some fifteen to twenty thousand Jews now awaiting deportation . . . [They] are being evacuated eastward into the war-devastated territory of the Ukraine under condi-tions so appalling that they would seem to afford a substantial share of the evacuees little chance to survive. . . . This modern Captivity would seem deliberately calculated to serve a pro-gram of virtual extermination. . . ."

Of the approximately 150,000 Jews deported to Transnistria, some 50,000 were still alive when the Soviets reconquered the area in March, 1944. Those who survived could not have done so without leaders such as Siegfried Jagendorf—the man who mastered the game of survival in the wilderness of exile.

ARON HIRT-MANHEIMER

*Part One*

---

# FALL, 1941

ARRIVAL IN TRANSNISTRIA

*Jagendorf Archives, Yad Vashem, The Holocaust Martyrs' and Heroes'*
*Remembrance Authority, Jerusalem*

# 1

## AN UNKNOWN DESTINATION

THE REPRESENTATIVE of the Jewish community of Radauti stood before the prefect as he announced the latest anti-Semitic decree: "All Jews must leave this city and relinquish their money, jewels, and securities to the National Bank. They may pack as much as they can carry, but no more than forty pounds. Houses must be left intact, keys in the doors. Within twenty-four hours all Jews must assemble at the railroad station. From there they will be transported to an unknown destination."

The Romanian authorities posted the expulsion edict throughout Radauti. On October 12, 1941, the city had to be emptied of Jews. Anyone failing to comply would be shot. For the more than 5,000 Jews whose families had dwelled there for generations, it was the darkest day of their lives. My only comforting thought was that our two married daughters had escaped to America.

The leaders of the Jewish community asked me to help organize the exodus, believing my executive experience and status as a former director of Siemens–Schukert Werke qualified me for the task. I recommended that we resist the decree. Let them kill us here, I said, on familiar ground. In that case, they cautioned, we would be shot and the people banished anyway.

I decided to cooperate with the edict after receiving assurances that no more than forty people would occupy each cattlecar. At departure time, however, the Romanians squeezed one hundred baggage-laden Jews into each unit. I protested, but all that mattered to them was their deadline. Romania could not tolerate our presence a moment longer.

Guarantees that families would be settled together on farms in the country proved equally spurious. At the very first station stop, sections of the train were detached and rerouted. Gendarmes tore husbands from wives, parents from children, plundering their possessions in the confusion. Our hastily-packed knapsacks commanded more value than our lives.

After a two-day journey, we detrained at Atachi, Bessarabia—the last station in Romania. We stood abandoned on the edge of exile. Seized by terror and anguish, parents fed their children poison tablets, then killed themselves. All around us people went insane.

Trains arrived in rapid succession, disgorging Jews from Bukovina like so much refuse. Ukrainian gangs competed with the Romanians in pillaging the deportees, wrenching rings from fingers, breaking arms and hands to extricate luggage. The Romanians set up a crude "customs office," where rapacious inspectors stripped Jews of valuables and documents. What possible use could Jews have for birth certificates or diplomas here?

The Dniester shoreline teemed with thousands of Jews waiting in desperation to board a primitive barge that would ferry them across the narrow waterway, fifteen to twenty per trip. The Romanian gendarmes waited for night to thrust their passengers into the icy water. Later, the bodies drifted back with the tide.

The morning after our arrival, a group of us from Radauti reached the eastern bank. We circumvented gendarmes who were forcing Jews into a barracks to be beaten and robbed. Afterwards, the victims were driven on foot to outlying areas: twenty, forty or more miles away. Any Jew lagging behind was shot on the spot. The roadside carnage would become a familiar sight in Transnistria.

Our little group entered the border city of Moghilev–Podolski unmolested. After finding shelter for Mrs. Jagendorf and the others, I set out alone to find the local German commander. With the aid of a letter identifying me as a former director of the giant German electrical company, Siemens–Schukert Werke, I eventually was ushered into the commander's office. I asked him what plans they had for us and where we might find some food and shelter. He replied, "The area between the Dniester and Bug Rivers is now under Romanian control. It is their responsibility to take care of deported Jews. As for food and water, you are on your own. I do not know where you will be sent, but I must warn you that Moghilev is off limits to Jews. There is nothing for you here. As you can see for yourself, the city is devastated. We are without electricity and other vital services. I can do nothing for you."

Our fate was in Romanian hands. They would squeeze us for every last drop of blood. We had to find a way to extend our usefulness or, better, to become indispensable. I remembered the commander's words: "The city is devastated . . . without electricity." A possible solution came to mind. We Jews could provide the technical expertise and manpower necessary to repair the power station, perhaps even rebuild the war-battered shops and factories of Transnistria's second largest city. But to do so, I would have to sell the idea to the prefect, the Romanian official who presided over the city and district of Moghilev.

In the meantime, I heard about an empty movie theater and applied at police headquarters for permission to use the building. I persuaded the besieged captain that confining several thousand Radauti Jews in one place would ease his task when our evacuation orders arrived. He agreed and instructed the guards at the dock to allow anyone I designated to follow me to the theater. I directed everyone to the shelter, whether from Radauti or not. When the building reached capacity, the police put several damaged houses at our disposal. At that moment, without fully realizing it, I had taken responsibility for the fate of Romania's banished Jews.

That night in the theater, huddled close to Hilda for warmth, I thought about the power station. Could the plant be repaired? I wanted to run outside and see for myself, but Moghilev at midnight was no place for a stateless Jew.

# 2

## THE PREFECT

O<small>N THE</small> second day, I walked to the prefectura and found myself among hundreds of Ukrainian petitioners waiting for an audience with the district's top Romanian official. I spent the day on the steps of the heavily guarded building, returned the following day, and the next, fearing we would be evacuated before the prefect received me. After two weeks, a sentry emerged from the building and called, "Jew Jagendorf." I followed him to the office of a young man in civilian attire. "Mr. Engineer," said the man behind the desk, "my name is Gheorghe Fuciu, the prefect's assistant. Please take a seat. Colonel Baleanu will be with you shortly."

Mr. Fuciu treated me politely, as though he did not realize I was a deportee. I did not look Jewish, and, although I slept on the floor of the theater with the rest, I shaved every day and wore a white shirt, a clean suit, and kid leather gloves. My dignity required no less. Whatever might happen, I resolved to address every official as an equal.

"Colonel Baleanu will see you now," announced Mr. Fuciu. As I entered, a tall man in uniform rose and greeted me with the well-known Viennese salutation: "Be greeted by the Lord," adding, "Yesterday we fought together. Shall I be your enemy today?" His effusive welcome caught me off guard.

*Authorization for the Jew, Engineer Max Schmit and four family members to remain in Moghilev to work in the Turnatoria. Written by Jagendorf's nephew Adalbert Regenstreif, dated November 10, 1941, signed by Gheorghe Fuciu, bears the stamp of the prefecture of Moghilev, valid until November 30, 1941. (courtesy of Max Schmidt)*

"Where did we fight together, Colonel Baleanu?"

"Engineer Jagendorf, I assume our paths must have crossed in the last war. You served as an officer in the Austrian army, did you not?"

"Yes I did, Mr. Prefect. I was a first lieutenant. You are the only official since the deportation to address me as a fellow human being."

I asked the colonel to join me at the window. He obliged. From our vantage point we witnessed a panorama of suffering and degradation: scores of people, mired in mud, overcome by hunger and exhaustion.

"Mr. Prefect, do you condone such treatment of innocent human beings for no reason other than they were born Jews?"

"No, I do not," he replied, returning to his desk. "But we shall not discuss it. I am not responsible for their condition. I am a soldier; a soldier must follow orders. Certainly you, Engineer Jagendorf, understand that."

Twice he had addressed me by my professional title. I decided to pursue my objectives.

"It is true that you must perform your duty, Mr. Prefect, but you also have a moral obligation to act humanely. History has placed upon your shoulders a great responsibility. You alone cannot change the course of events, but you can do something to alleviate the suffering."

"What do you have in mind?"

"Restrain the gendarmes who are raping our women, beating our men, stealing everything. And provide us with food; our provisions have run out."

"Engineer Jagendorf, you must realize that Jews cannot stay in Moghilev; we are establishing camps for them elsewhere in the district. As for food, I cannot help you."

I was weighing in my mind whether to propose the idea of putting Jewish professionals at the prefect's disposal, when Colonel Baleanu said, "Now, I'll tell you why I granted you this audience. We need your services here in Moghilev. The power station was incapacitated during the siege and further damaged when the Dniester overflowed its banks. I want you to select a few electricians and mechanics from your ranks, four or five perhaps. You will also need a machine shop, which you have my consent to appropriate for this purpose. I do not believe they will hang me for permitting a handful of Jews to remain in the city." I assured the colonel that we would fulfill his every expectation.

Returning to the theater, I thought about the prefect's offer to authorize four or five men. But hundreds of Jews needed protection. Perhaps that would come; for the moment, at least, I had secured a Jewish foothold in Moghilev.

# 3

# THE TURNATORIA

I ENLISTED SEVERAL young men to scout the city for an abandoned machine shop. They discovered a large foundry and metal fittings factory near the river. After receiving authorizations to inspect the guarded compound, five of us entered the largest building. It was a depressing sight: the roof collapsing, windows shattered, walls crumbling, floors covered with debris. We examined the diesel generator, the lathes and punch presses, all sabotaged by the retreating Soviets in a hasty effort to render them useless. The five of us stood silently, weighing the odds, balancing the alternatives. I closed my eyes and imagined the bustle of hundreds of Jews working, machines turning, products moving. Then I announced, "We will rebuild it!" The date was November 3, 1941.

I rushed with the news to Colonel Baleanu. He wanted to inspect the facility without delay and invited me to accompany him in his automobile. Never shall I forget the look of astonishment on the faces of the Jews when they saw me in the back seat with the prefect of Moghilev.

Together we walked through each building, checking the machines and taking an inventory of raw material. The prefect finally turned to me and said, "I doubt that even you can make anything of this mess. And don't forget, the winter here is severe and long."

"We will succeed," I assured him, "if we have at least one hundred men."

"Are you mad? I told you that Jews cannot stay here. I made an exception in your case, only because the German commander agreed to look the other way. He'll never go along with this."

"Mr. Prefect, the job cannot be done with only four or five men. We will need a managerial committee to properly control the project, and dozens of skilled workers to craft the tools necessary for repairing the machines. I assure you there is no other way to restore the city's power. Approve my request, Mr. Prefect; nobody will fault you for forcing a few Jews to work for the state."

As I expected, the Colonel Ion Baleanu chose expediency over propriety. He instructed Mr. Fuciu to issue the authorizations and commanded the factory guards to obey my instructions. At that moment I could hardly restrain my exhilaration. But walking back to the theater, I was struck by doubt. The specter of the factory's gaping ceilings and disemboweled motors filled me with despair. Without tools, how could we replace machine parts? The authorities would regard failure as a hoax, as proof of our obsolescence. I feared my pact with the prefect spelled doom, not deliverance.

In the theater, Hilda told me that the people were saying I had gone insane. Maybe it was crazy to think that these Jews could rise above their misery and create a miracle. I convinced myself that the factory, which we called the Turnatoria (foundry in Romanian) was our only hope.

The next day we established a hiring office and began looking for skilled craftsmen and professionals. A crowd of applicants besieged us. We scrutinized them, weeding out the unqualified. Candidates had to demonstrate proficiency in their field, whether in carpentry, bookkeeping, electronics, or locksmithing. We also tried to identify Jewish informers recruited by various authorities to infiltrate the Turnatoria. At stake was our credibility; we had to avoid even a hint of impropriety, especially with the Germans watching us from the sidelines.

In the evening I met Mr. Fuciu at the prefectura and handed him a list of 116 names. Then I raised the question of their family members, explaining that they too would need permission to remain in Moghilev. We could not expect much productivity from men who lived in dread of their loved ones being hauled off to some Lager (forced labor or concentration camp). He concurred and asked me to return the next day with a roster of the workers' relatives. Each man claimed ten or more dependents. Mr. Fuciu had no way of verifying the information because border guards had confiscated their documents. At final tally, I held authorizations for nearly 1,200 people!

The prefect agreed to billet the workers and their families in a school building near the Turnatoria. We repaired the roof and windows, using salvage from the city's abundant stock of bombed-out houses. Each classroom accommodated about thirty people. Our carpenters constructed partitions, lofts, and bunkbeds to compartmentalize the tight quarters. Our staff of engineers occupied a separate building that formerly housed Ukrainian factory employees. Additional buildings were requisitioned and remodeled to absorb the overflow. We established a special commission to ensure an equitable distribution of the limited space, appointed an administrator at each house to maintain strict discipline and to mediate disputes between residents. A watchman enforced curfews and barred unauthorized guests.

Clean-up operations took precedence in the Turnatoria. Architect Samuel Kurzweil uncovered a large cache of raw materials—sheet metal, bronze, coke, and lumber—that the fleeing Russians had concealed beneath a junk pile. In a sheltered corner of one of the Turnatoria structures, a team of blacksmiths and toolmakers fashioned implements from scrap metal. Another team rummaged the city for reusable roofing materials, glass, and lumber. Some of our men, too weak to work, could do little more than lie on the factory floor. We lacked the food and medicine to save them.

We sectioned the Turnatoria into five departments, each headed by an experienced professional: Architect Samuel Kurzweil in architecture and construction; Engineer Leo Litmann in foundry and casting; Engineer Max Schmidt in the lathe and power plant; Engineer Joseph Morgenstern in lock-smithing; and Engineer Leopold Rauch in the punch press and toolshop. Pinkas Katz, the general superintendent, supervised the overall work of the Turnatoria and procured the necessary materials. He reported directly to me.

Having no other skilled workers at his disposal, the prefect ordered us to supply a crew of carpenters and an architect to aid in the construction of a wooden bridge over the Dniester. Short of carpenters, we sent novices. Who couldn't learn to use a hammer and a saw if his life depended on it? Fortunately, the on-site officer proved decent. He was sufficiently grateful for the extra hands to overlook their occasional clumsiness.

All the while, a team of our electrical engineers and mechanics worked on the municipal power station, completing the repairs in less than two weeks. When I announced the achievement to the prefect, he stared at me in disbelief. In the days that followed, we ran electricity to the post office, secret service headquarters, and to the Turnatoria. The three-month power blackout of Moghilev ended with the rekindling of the electric street lights. I was the talk of the town.

The Germans acquired additional information about me from a soldier stationed in Moghilev whose father had been my chauffeur when I worked for Siemens–Schukert in Vienna. I also met a German lieutenant who was the son of a Siemens–Schukert engineer in my department. Several Romanians remembered me from my days with the company in Cernauti. All these connections reinforced my image as a competent corporate manager.

The authorities ordered us to repair the city's damaged government buildings, beginning with the offices of the prefectura and police. I requested hundreds of additional authorizations, which Colonel Baleanu now signed routinely. The prefect commanded an army of slaves, ready to do his bidding in exchange for nothing more than rubber-stamped slips of paper that affirmed our tenuous link to civilization.

# 4

## ORDINANCE NO. 23

By MID-NOVEMBER, the authorities stopped speaking of Moghilev as a city closed to Jews. We made every effort to create new jobs for as many deportees as possible, despite the near absence of food and housing. We also hired local Jews, who had shared with us their meager food supply, consisting primarily of a thin leafy soup and course bread.

To secure additional authorizations, I offered to provide the Ukrainian mayor, Alexander Ivanov, with workers to clean up and repair the roads and to collect refuse. He hated Jews, but since the prefect and the German commander seemed to be making themselves fat off of us, why shouldn't he? Ivanov's request for authorizations was granted by the prefect, allowing us to keep even more Jews in the city.

Moghilev had a lumber mill, which, like everything else, had been laid waste. Although, at the time, there was no possibility of floating lumber down the Dniester to feed the mill, I requested and received authorizations for Jewish workers to repair the installation.

We also helped rebuild Moghilev's crippled flour mills and wineries, the principal processing centers of the fertile Dniester valley. The Germans needed little convincing that restoration of food production in the district could alleviate food shortages on the battle front.

If it appears that we were working for the enemy, we must ask: who was our enemy—the Germans and Romanians who annihilate us today or the Russians who would enslave us tomorrow? The enemy was death itself, and our only business survival.

By this time, more than 10,000 Jews were engaged in productive labor, but none of them received a single RKKS mark (*Reichskreditkassenscheine*—German occupation scrip) in return. Our people were forced to barter their clothes for food and risk death from exposure; those who clung to their clothes starved. Whole families dropped from sight, their frozen remains undetected until the spring thaw, when the stench choked Moghilev. I decided to request authorizations for professionals and tradesmen who could bring us a modicum of comfort. We needed doctors, dentists, barbers, tailors, cooks, shoemakers. Colonel Baleanu resisted the request, complaining that his superiors in Odessa, the capital of Transnistria, and the Germans already suspected him of being a Jew-lover.

"I must put an end to this kind of thinking," he said, "for your sake and mine."

"Mr. Prefect," I said, "look what we have done for the city in so short a time. Our continued presence here is tolerated only because of our contributions, not out of compassion or kindness."

"Yes, but it does not change the fact that my troubles are increasing in proportion to your contributions. In our mutual interest, I ask that you get along without these additional people."

"I do not believe that your approving my request will change the status quo. Follow the German saying: 'Do the right thing and be not frightened.' Be assured, Mr. Prefect, we will never forget all you have done on our behalf. For us, these authorizations mean life or death; for you, it is a matter of possibly being reassigned. Of course, losing you would be a great blow to us. I will do my best to enhance your status by complaining at every opportunity about your cruelty."

Colonel Baleanu approved the authorizations with great reluctance. A few days later, he invited me to a meeting attended by the heads of all city departments and several German observers. The prefect reviewed existing reconstruction projects and specified additional goals. At the end of the meeting he named me coordinator of public works. I took the opportunity to protest the colonel's unreasonable demand that Jews labor in the cold for long hours, receiving no food rations, coats, heating fuel, or shelter. I complained that even animals are not sent into the fields with empty stomachs. The prefect retorted, "I have received no order to compensate Jews."

We could no more count on the native Ukrainians for sympathy and support than we could on the Romanians or Germans. Our people were savaged and murdered daily without recourse. Our legal status remained undefined until November 11, 1941, when Marshal Ion Antonescu and Transnistria's governor, Gheorghe Alexianu, signed Ordinance No. 23, a series of laws that established Transnistria as a penal colony, divided into thirteen districts. The ordinance granted the exiles "opportunities for labor" and self-administration, while severely curtailing our movement. Jews caught outside their assigned domicile risked summary execution as spies. The ordinance stipulated that each camp and ghetto install a Jewish chief who would be held responsible for implementing all administrative and police orders. Every Jew was obliged to register with the Romanian authorities and carry at all times a certificate listing name, nationality, religion, age, profession, and place of origin.

Ordinance No. 23 entitled tradesmen and professionals to work in their areas of expertise and receive as compensation 2 RKKS marks (sixty cents) for a day's work. Unskilled workers were to receive 1 RKKS mark per work day for tasks such as repairing roads, removing rubble, and clearing forests. With government approval, Jewish specialists could work in essential manufacturing enterprises.

# 5

## THE JEWISH
## COMMITTEE

On November 18, 1941, a week after the enactment of Ordinance No. 23, Gheorghe Culnev, subprefect of Moghilev, issued a protocol listing the names of a thirteen-member committee to coordinate Jewish labor in the district. He warned us that any committee member failing to implement government orders would be punished severely. The committee included nine individuals recommended by representatives of their home communities—Siegfried Jagendorf (engineer), Feiwel Laufer (lumber industrialist), Simon Hilsenrad (superior judge), Dr. Jonas Kessler (attorney), Dr. Meyer Teich (attorney), Isidor Pressner (president of the Radauti Jewish community), Moritz Klipper, Moses Katz (engineer), and Emanuel Wolfsohn (engineer). We added Leon Schafler, Abraham Fleischer, Hermann Kastner, and Leon Varsinger at the request of the prefect. We learned that they had been charging Jews exorbitant fees to arrange transportation to the outlying lagers and sharing the profits with the prefect. Considering how helpful Colonel Baleanu had been to me and to the deportees in general, I felt obliged to add the names of the four to the committee list.

On November 23, I sent the prefect the first in a series of letters urging the cessation of further evacuations until suitable transportation could be arranged, especially for the old people, children, and the infirm. I also requested food and fuel, insisting that the committee could not take responsibility for organizing the evacuations if these conditions were not met. Appealing to the colonel's humanitarian instincts, I won several short delays, allowing us to obtain additional authorizations and to arrange conveyance for those unable to remain in Moghilev.

Mayor Alexander Ivanov managed a fleet of German supply trucks that were used to bring provisions from the countryside. I asked him if the empty outbound trucks could be used to transport Jews to the Lager. "For a price, it can be arranged," he said. I paused. Officially we were not allowed to possess money. If we were caught paying off the mayor, the punishment would be severe. But measured against the number of lives that could be saved, I considered the risk worth taking.

"I do not know where we will find the money," I said, "but we will find it."

The mayor smiled and said, "Don't trouble yourself about the fee now, so long as it comes in due course."

The following day, people began signing up for a place on the trucks. Those who had managed to hide their money had to subsidize the destitute. We could not allow a privileged few to ride, while the rest froze to death along the way. A special committee worked out the financial details, drawing communal funds when needed.

At the first meeting of the Jewish Committee, I was asked to serve as president. I refused, insisting that I was an engineer, not an administrator, and that building up the Turnatoria kept me busy enough. The members rejected my refusal, calling it a betrayal. They argued that I was obligated to accept the position because the authorities had confidence in me. But I was loathe to head a committee that included racketeers who could not be counted on to do the work for which we would be held accountable. After a long and heated discussion, I agreed to serve as interim chief on condition that we try to recruit Dr. Meyer Teich for the job. I recommended Mr. Feiwel Laufer, an excellent man, as vice president.

Dr. Teich was a well-known attorney who had served as president of the Jewish community in his native Suceava. I obtained an authorization for Dr. Teich to visit from the Sargorod Lager, about twenty miles north of Moghilev. I offered him the position but he refused, choosing to remain as the Jewish chief in Sargorod. He explained:

"I feel it would be a crime against the deported Jews in this county for me to assume the title. I can well understand that the problems of Turnatoria are burdensome and that you prefer to separate committee from technical responsibilities, but I believe it is in the common Jewish interest for you to act as our leader. If you need my help, I am prepared to move to Moghilev."

I did not expect to hear this response from Dr. Teich, a man reputed to be vain and ambitious. Unable to sway him, I accepted his offer of help and made relocation arrangements for him, his wife, and their twenty-year-old son. Dr. Teich changed his mind after returning to Sargorod. In my opinion, he had made a great mistake, even though he believed he could be more valuable to his people by remaining in the Lager. His only son died of a liver condition, exacerbated by malnutrition and the cold. Following the funeral, both parents took poison. Mrs. Teich died and was placed in the grave with her son. Dr. Teich remained in Sargorod, where he would be unjustly imprisoned when the Soviets retook the area.

After Dr. Teich refused to become committee president, I placated my colleagues and accepted the office. My first priority was to purge the four traitors. I went to see Major Danulescu, commander of the gendarme legion in Moghilev. Knowing full well why the prefect had placed his business associates on the committee, the major backed my effort. He asked me to draw up a written proposal, which he handed personally to Colonel Baleanu. The prefect responded by withdrawing his support for the four, who, in any case, were no longer of any use to him because the committee was now arranging transportation for the evacuees. Colonel Baleanu approved our reconstituted committee in January, 1942.

*Commentary for Part One*

---

# Fall, 1941

ROMANIA ENTERED World War II in July, 1941 as an ally of the Germans in the surprise attack on the Soviet Union, code-named Operation Barbarossa. Within weeks, German and Romanian forces recovered the "lost provinces" of Bessarabia and northern Bukovina (which the Soviets had seized the previous summer) and occupied a large portion of the Soviet Ukraine. As the fascist armies rolled across the Soviet territory, they were accompanied by special units charged with the liquidation of all Jewish civilians, commissars, and Communists within reach. The German mobile killing units, the Einstazgruppen, had a Romanian counterpart called the Special Echelon. Both relied heavily on local informers and collaborators. When no natural ravines or cliffs were available, the killing units forced the victims to dig their own graves, strip naked, and stand along the edge. The shootings continued until the city or village was declared *Judenrein* (cleansed or free of Jews). According to the International Military Tribunal at Nuremberg, the Einsatzgruppen were ordered to liquidate Jews "without truce, without investigation, without pity, tears, or remorse. Women were to be slain with men, and the children were to be executed because, otherwise, they would grow up to oppose National Socialism and might even nurture a desire to avenge themselves on the slayers of their parents."

Einsatzgruppen gunners murdered more than 1.25 million Russian Jews. Romanian security forces, army troops, gendarmes, police, and the civil administration participated zealously in the killings, spearheading the extermination of at least 250,000 Jews in the Old Kingdom, Bessarabia, Bukovina, and in the Ukraine. Historian Raul Hilberg has said of Romania, "No country, besides Germany, was involved in the massacre of Jews on such a scale."

———————

The war in Europe had been raging for two years before it reached Siegfried Jagendorf and the Jews of Radauti in October 1941. The Germans already had conquered and overrun Poland, Denmark, Norway, Holland, Belgium, Luxembourg, France, Greece, and Yugoslavia. It had taken only weeks for combined German and Romanian forces to demolish Soviet fortifications in Bessarabia, northern Bukovina, and the southern Ukraine.

Historically, Jews had commanded a central role in the commercial and cultural life of Radauti (pronounced Rah-däh-oots). Jews had first arrived in this market town at the end of the eighteenth century from Bohemia and later from Galicia and Russia. In the interwar period, the Jews of Radauti had been embroiled in the religious and political ferment that existed throughout Bukovina, with Zionists, Socialists, Hasidim, and other factions passionately defending conflicting visions of Jewish redemption. The official Jewish communal structure, the Gemeinde, maintained contact with the Romanian government and with the Union of Jewish Communities, based in Bucharest and headed since 1923 by Dr. Wilhelm Filderman.

During the months preceding the deportation edict, the Jewish leadership of Radauti found itself responsible for several thousand Jews who had been expelled from nearby villages and concentrated in the town to be exploited as slave labor by Romanian military and civil authorities. Siegfried Jagendorf, who had no experience in political or Jewish communal affairs, offered to organize a Jewish labor office in Radauti as a means of averting brutal and indiscriminate street roundups by local police and gendarmes. To keep families together and protect the forced laborers from being evacuated to distant Lager, Jagendorf convinced the Romanian officials that it would be in their own best interest to utilize the free labor at home rather than export it elsewhere.

This achievement demonstrated Jagendorf's ability to deal effectively with the Romanians. The failed businessman asserted his leadership in the Jewish community and soon rivaled the Gemeinde president, Isidor (Eisig) Pressner. Only two weeks before the deportations, Jagendorf sent Dr. Wilhelm Filderman birthday greetings on stationery of the Radauti Gemeinde and signed his name above the title, "acting president."

The expulsion decree took the approximately 6,500 Jews of Radauti (about one-third of the town's total population) by surprise because southern Bukovina had never been under Soviet domination and was not in a battle zone. Nevertheless, Ion Antonescu spread his fury over the whole of Bukovina, ordering the expulsion of Jews from the province, with the exception of an "indispensable" few. In Radauti, for instance, the only gynecologist and the only dentist were among those exempted.

Soon after the deportation decree was announced, Gemeinde president Pressner won two concessions from the prefect of Radauti: each Jew would be permitted to take 2,000 lei ($10) and all the luggage he or she could carry with no weight limit. Jagendorf attempted to secure humane travel conditions for the deportees, but, according to his nephew, Adalbert Regenstreif, succeeded only for himself, his relatives, and several of the town's most prominent Jews. This elite group made the two-day voyage to Transnistria in a relatively uncrowded cattle car.

The four Radauti transports were split and rerouted in Lipcani, Bessarabia; two trains were sent to Moghilev-Podolski (Moh-ghee-lev Poh-dohl-skee) via Atachi (Ah-tah-kee) and the others to Bersad, near the Bug (Boog) River, Transnistria's eastern boundry. The deportees had no advance knowledge of their destination. Only upon reaching the shore of the Dniester (Dnee-es-ter) River, delineating the Ukrainian border, did they realize the full magnitude of their tragedy.

Dr. Meyer Teich, the leader of the Suceava (Soo-chah-vah) Jews, who would reject Jagendorf's offer to head the Jewish Committee in Moghilev, chronicled the scene at the border:

"We arrived in Atachi, or more precisely in the place where it once existed. . . . As a result of the bombardment, all houses were burned down or ruined. Walls with holes in them, here and there a roof or a part of a roof, blood and mud, everywhere traces of the pogrom that destroyed the entire Jewish community of this place; everywhere corpses in the streets, yards, cellars. On many a wall were inscriptions: 'You who will come here, say a *Kaddish* (prayer of mourning)' or 'We died for the *Kiddush Hashem* (sanctification of God's name) or 'Here was murdered . . . with all his family.'

"The gravely sick and aged with no family were placed in a house which had no doors or windows, only a dry floor and a roof. After nightfall I visited my aunt, Golda Breiner, an 87-year-old woman. . . . Beside her on the floor lay her husband Shaye Langer, over 90, one of the most respected businessmen of Bukovina, who still prided himself on that fact that he was one of the delegates to the first Zionist Congress in Basel . . . His wife whispered to him that I was there and he asked me to step nearer. I knelt down beside him. He grasped my hand and held it clasped in trembling fingers for a long time. For a while he couldn't talk, the tears stifling his voice; then he gathered himself and said: 'Dear Doctor, how is it possible that they drive me away from Suceava? I was born there ninety years ago. I lived and worked there. I took over my father's store and ran it for sixty years. I had been imperial councillor, city councillor, leader of the congregation. I've never fought with anyone and was honored and liked by all. You must promise me that you'll send memoranda to all competent authorities explaining to them all I told you. Ask them to send us back, me and my wife, as we are two old people. In Suceava we have already prepared the graves for both of us. They should permit us to die there. . . .' Within an hour he expired. I buried him on the Dniester's bank. . . ."

The deportees from southern Bukovina arrived in good condition compared to those from Bessarabia who came by foot. Dr. Teich remembered a convoy of Bessarabian Jews marching through Atachi from the Edineti (Ee-din-ehtz) concentration camp:

"Never shall I forget this scene. They are no longer human beings. Hungry, clad in rags, they drag themselves, tremble, moan, yell. In the bottom of their eyes is the fear of death, even as in the eyes of hunted animals fleeing before a pack of hounds amid whining bullets. This herd of beaten men . . . march in a uniform, almost unconscious motion. The beasts permit no rest, driving them forward in the direction of the Dniester, the raft, the inferno. We surround them and in a split second of confusion succeed in slipping into their hands some food and clothing. We hide some of them in our ranks. The soldiers quickly break up our cordon, and I hear for the first time: 'Whoever lags behind will be shot dead!' I was to hear this all too often. . . ."

The Romanian border police at Atachi, intoxicated with greed, plundered the deportees mercilessly. An investigation of lieutenant Augustin Rosca of police platoon #60 conducted by the General Inspectorate of the Gendarmes noted the following:

"His wife, a school teacher, travels frequently to Atachi and returns . . . carrying heavy suitcases. . . . Lt. Rosca has taken valuables from Jews without making any lists or giving receipts, simply putting everything into his pockets. The same holds true for the other leaders of the platoon. . . . We know that he has taken gold from Jews by the kilogram, as well as dollars and other objects of value. He also has taken their suitcases and deposited them in a storehouse.

"The Jews could take with them only what they were wearing, but no money. . . . A loaf of bread was sold to the Jews for 500 lei ($2.50), a slice for 100 lei ($.50), and a container of milk for 600 lei ($3.00).

"According to the post office in Atachi, leaders of the police platoon mail packages of money to their homes. . . . All the officers have valuable objects in their apartments.

"It is alleged that Lt. Rosca has said that he will retire at the war's end because he has enough money to live on."

Isidor Pressner, president of the Radauti Gemeinde, managed to send an SOS from Atachi to Dr. Filderman in Bucharest:

"You have surely heard the news that on October 14 we were all brought here to be ferried across the Dniester and sent somewhere in the Ukraine without any real aim or destination. . . . The majority remain under the open sky in the rain and cold. . . . Hundreds of persons have already died here. Many have gone mad; others have killed themselves. . . . One thing is certain, if we are not rescued immediately, no one will survive this misfortune."

Dr. Meyer Teich of Suceava reported that he and other Jewish leaders from various southern Bukovina communities made contact in Atachi and held a strategy meeting. The group consisted of Dr. Jonas Kessler of Vatra Dornei, Dr. Josef Schauer of Campulung, Feiwel Laufer of Gura-Humora, Jagendorf and Pressner of Radauti. Teich recounted:

"We had in our hands a detailed report of conditions across the Dniester. People are robbed on the ferry and often thrown overboard. Upon reaching the other side they are brought to a dilapidated building called the Casino and at night are arbitrarily regrouped with no regard for the preservation of families. The formations then are marched north without plan or purpose. Their guards beat and rob them along the way. Some groups reach Ozarineti, Copaigorod, and Bar but find neither food nor housing. In

Atachi one ruble is exchanged for forty lei; across the river one receives only six to eight lei. In Moghilev the local Jews suffer great hardships and cannot be expected to help."

According to Teich, Dr. Jonas Kessler responded to the report by calling for active resistance as the only honorable solution to the hopeless situation. The majority rejected Kessler's argument.

In Teich's words:

"Without arms and with a mass of confused and discouraged people who would not follow us in revolt, we could inflict no harm whatsoever on the enemy. In the end, the leaders would be brought before firing squads, and, stripped of leadership, the deportees would die in agony."

Teich reported that the Jewish communal leaders in Atachi collected a large quantity of money and precious objects from several wealthy deportees and in an undisclosed manner secreted the assets across the Dniester. The leaders charged a fee for this service, ranging from two to ten percent and totalling 3.5 million lei ($17,500). The money formed the basis for a communal aid fund that was administered by a five-person committee. Teich revealed no further details.

Siegfried Jagendorf (Yay-gen-dorf), it seems, had achieved top leadership status among the deportees even before his arrival in Moghilev. At the meeting of community heads in Atachi, the engineer gained advance knowledge of the conditions he would encounter in Transnistria, and he probably had access to the 3.5 million lei aid fund.

---

Moghilev–Podolski was the gateway to Transnistria for nearly 60,000 exiled Romanian Jews from September, 1941 to February, 1942. Situated in a fertile valley amid jutting hills, this border city in the region formerly known as Podolia had served for centuries as a way station on the trade route between the Ukraine and Moldavia (part of the Old Kingdom of Romania). The city's Jewish population, which dated from 1638, grew to more than 12,000 by 1897. A wave of pogroms in 1905 and the closing of Jewish religious institutions following the Bolshevik revolution resulted in a sharp decline. In 1926 census showed 9,622 Jews in Moghilev, almost 42 percent of the city's total population.

German and Romanian troops overran the city on July 19, 1941. According to an Einsatzgruppe field report to Berlin on August 3, 1941, "In Moghilev–Podolski no operation is necessary since the Russians have evacuated the entire population and devastated the town completely." The Jewish men of military age most likely were drafted into the Red Army; some may have joined the resistance. The majority of Jewish women, children, and the elderly presumably fell victim to the killing units of Einsatzgruppe D, which accompanied the German Eleventh Army. According to Jagendorf, approximately 3,000 Jewish survivors returned to Moghilev and reoccupied the ruins of what had been their homes.

Their abject poverty notwithstanding, the Jews of Moghilev shared their meager food supply with the exiles. The generosity of the besieged Ukrainian Jews was not unique to Moghilev. Dr. Avigdor Shachan reports in his study of the ghettos in Transnistria that the Jews of Lucineti (Lu-sen-etz) met the exiles with loaves of bread and bowls of soup and obtained police permission to quarter the newcomers in their cramped homes. Their coreligionists reciprocated, but less than ten percent of the approximately 300,000 Ukrainian Jews in Transnistria survived the occupation.

---

By his own account, when Siegfried Jagendorf arrived in Moghilev, he made contact with the German commandant and asked for information regarding the disposition of Jews. Adalbert Regenstreif, the nephew who accompanied the Jagendorfs to Transnistria, reports that his uncle had dressed in his Romanian officer's uniform before venturing out that first day in Moghilev. To obtain information from the Germans Jagendorf may have posed as a non-Jewish reserve lieutenant. (He had been demobilized on September 2, 1940, in accordance with the purge of Jews from the Romanian military.) If the engineer had been caught impersonating an officer, he would most likely have been summarily executed as a spy. Nonetheless, Jagendorf had considered the risk worth taking.

---

Shortly before Jagendorf's first tête-à-tête with the prefect, a group of prominent Radauti Jews had sent the following letter to Colonel Baleanu:

"Mister Prefect,

"The undersigned, heads of families evacuated from the town of Radauti . . . petition you to kindly provide transportation for 250 persons. . . . We commit ourselves to pay in advance for the necessary . . . eight trucks.

"We want to stress that our group includes representatives of almost all civil professions (doctors, pharmacists, technicians, artisans, farmers, and industrialists); therefore it is possible for us immediately to effect the restoration of the location you designate for us.

"The members of our group have been loyal citizens of good reputation, hard working people and appreciated by the authorities of Radauti. And we can assure you, Sir, . . . we shall respect to your utmost satisfaction all the orders given by you and the local authorities.

"For the reasons mentioned we respectfully repeat our request . . . kindly allot us a suitable locality and approve the . . . eight trucks. Please, Mister Prefect, accept the assurance of our deepest respect and consideration."

The letter was signed by Dr. G. Preminger, M. Bitter, and Pinkas Katz, among others, who soon would play key roles on Jagendorf's Jewish Committee and in the Turnatoria. On October 28, 1941, Colonel Baleanu penned two notations at the top of the hand-written petition. The first, in Romanian, stated, "Upon their request, I agree to intervene with the German authorities. [Signed] Prefect Col. Baleanu." The second notation, written in German, stated, "Upon request, I approve the petitioners' bid to the German authorities to permit . . . transportation from here to Copaigorod (Ko-pie-goh-rohd) [Signed] Royal Romanian Prefect of Moghilev Col. Baleanu." The fact that the prefect could write in German indicates that he, too, came from the German-speaking Bukovina (which had been part of Austro-Hungary before the Allies awarded it to Romania following the first world war.) It appears that both Baleanu and Jagendorf had served as officers in the Austrian army and retained their rank after becoming citizens of Romania. That the engineer and prefect shared a common background was acknowledged in the manner Col. Baleanu had greeted Jagendorf: "Yesterday we fought together. Shall I be your enemy today?"

The letter cited above supports the assertion that the prefect was taking payments for arranging transportation to Lager elsewhere in the district. It also shows that, while the elite of Radauti had accepted the inevitability of evacuation from Moghilev, Jagendorf privately pursued the initiative that would open the border city to Jewish colonization. The Turnatoria began operations only five days after the prefect had assigned the 250 petitioners to Copaigorod. The letters' signatories either never went to the lager or they returned to Moghilev at Jagendorf's request.

---

One of the prefect's four Jewish business partners purged by Jagendorf from Moghilev's first Jewish Committee was Leon Varsinger. In 1947, the state attorney's office of the Romanian People's Republic investigated Varsinger and, after hearing the testimony summarized below, recommended prosecution for war crimes:

"Leon Varsinger, fifty years old . . . is accused by Jonas Lipp, one of the deportees in Moghilev, of taking 3,000 lei ($15), six gold rings, and a gold bracelet to intervene (with the authorities) so that (Jonas Lipp) be sent to Copaigorod, where supposedly the Jews were treated more humanely than in other Lager. . . . Betti Scherzer [testified] that her father gave Varsinger 75,000 lei ($375) for transportation to a Lager. After taking the money, the accused broke his promises. Betti Scherzer's father fell ill and asked Varsinger to return a small portion of the money needed for medical purposes. The accused refused, resulting in Mr. Scherzer's death. . . . The witness Mendel Welman paid Varsinger 210,000 lei ($1,050) to be transferred to Djurin with his entire family. . . . Varsinger promised to send Alter Rosenkranz to another Lager for 11,000 lei [$55], a gold ring, and a second ring with three jewels. Despite all this, the accused left him in Moghilev."

Baleanu and his subprefects Gheorghe Culnev and Alexandre Moisev were investigated by the Gendarme Inspectorate of Transnistria on March 22, 1942, and stripped of office several weeks later. The investigation revealed that the prefect and his deputies charged the deportees 50,000 lei ($250) for each German truck, even though the Germans had been transporting Jews without charge, and 40,000 lei ($200) for each prefecture truck. The operation yielded a total of 5,209,000 lei ($26,045). The funds were laundered through the mayor's office as funds for the purchase of equipment to be used in municipal restoration projects. It appeared, however, that a considerable sum had been withdrawn by the prefecture cabinet chief, Gheorghe Butnaru, who had disappeared from Moghilev. The prefecture used part of the funds to purchase an automobile for Colonel Baleanu. The report also noted that the colonel used a 100,000 lie ($500) "contribution" from a group of Jews to decorate a Christmas tree.

On November 25, 1941, three weeks after Jagendorf discovered the Turnatoria, Mihail Danilof and Yanko Marcu, leaders of the deported Jews from the district of Dorohoi (Dohr-o-hoy) made a "donation" of 500,000 lei ($2,500) to Subprefect Moisev for authorizing 649 individuals to remain in the city as workers. After receiving payment, the subprefect provided Danilof and Marcu with blank authorizations, which Moisev signed after they had been filled in by the Dorohoi leaders.

Danilof, an attorney from the Old Kingdom of Romania (Moldavia and Wallachia), viewed bribery as a fact of life. Siegfried Jagendorf, whose sensibilities were more Austrian than Romanian, considered bribery demeaning and politically unwise. The engineer preferred to operate on a much grander scale, impressing the authorities with the profit potential of disciplined workers in factories and trade shops.

---

According to a report in the Jagendorf Archives, the factory that Jagendorf considered the Jews' best hope for survival had been built in 1892 by a Jew. The czarist government appropriated the plant during the first world war, and it was temporarily closed after the Bolshevik revolution. In 1935, at the pinacle of its productivity, the factory employed 250 workers to produce replacement valves for farm equipment used in the surrounding kolkhozes (collective farms). At the beginning of November, 1941, it became an instrument of salvation for the deported Jews.

Siegfried Jagendorf, his brother-in-law Moritz Langberg, nephew Adalbert Regenstreif and Engineers Max Schmidt and Joseph Morgenstern entered the Turnatoria for the first time on November 3, 1941. The scene was dismal—machine parts and broken glass strewn about, rusted iron in moss-covered heaps, a gray sky visible through the ceiling. Max Schmidt recalled in an interview that they were standing among the sabotaged lathes when Jagendorf turned to him and asked, "Can we do it?" Schmidt replied, "We cannot, but we must." Jagendorf then said emphatically, "We will do it."

First, they needed to recruit specialists and skilled workers, a difficult task because the exiles had been dispersed haphazardly to far-flung lagers and forbidden to leave them. Of the 116 workers initially chosen, many had no industrial experience and had to be trained. Max Schmidt estimated that sixty to seventy skilled Turnatoria workers led by five engineers protected some 3,000 people.

News of the Turnatoria spread quickly to the Lager. Herman Sattinger, a foundry specialist from Cernauti (Cher-notes), was confined to the Copaigorod Lager when he learned about the Jewish-run facility. Despite the peril of leaving the Lager, the Sattingers embarked on a thirty-mile trek back to Moghilev, skirting gendarme patrols and Ukrainian bandits. Sattinger told me in Yiddish what happened to him when he reached Moghilev:

"We entered the city at night to avoid the guards. There was no sign of life. We camped in an abandoned house, where my wife and young son rested while I searched for the foundry. Soon I heard a voice coming from a building and followed the sound. I peeked through a pile of rubble barricading a doorway and recognized a man who in Cernauti had owned a bake shop. He waved me in and warned me not to go back into the street because people were being grabbed for forced labor. I waited two hours before venturing out. Someone called out my name. I looked around and spotted the former bookkeeper of my foundry in Cernauti. He offered to introduce me to an engineer who worked for Siegfried Jagendorf.

"In the morning, heading for the foundry, I suddenly felt a strong hand on the back of my neck. I turned around and saw that my assailant was wearing a Jewish police armband. Before I could say a word, he dragged me like a dog to the train station and forced me to join twenty or thirty men loading lumber onto a freight car. I managed to escape and rejoined my family.

"The next day I reached the factory without incident. At the gate I was greeted by a number of locksmiths, shoemakers, and other tradespeople whom I knew from Cernauti. We started talking, when one of them suddenly whispered, 'Look, here comes Jagendorf.' Everyone regarded him with reverence, as if the kaiser had arrived. I walked up to Engineer Jagendorf and introduced myself. 'You are Sattinger,' he said with a look of surprise. 'We sent gendarmes to Copaigorod to fetch you after hearing you were there. We need you.' 'If I had waited until the gendarmes came for me,' I said, 'there would have been no one to bring back.' "

After Jagendorf was appointed director of the Turnatoria on November 10, 1941, he moved into a four-room house at 65 Ermana Street, which he and Hilda shared with the Regenstreifs (Siegfried's sister Mina and family) and with the Langbergs (Hilda's sister Rosa and family). The other Turnatoria employees and their relatives were concentrated in a large school building, four or five families to a room. A nearby ghetto housed approximately 10,000 deportees who obtained authorizations through bribery and other means, including forgery and prostitution. In addition, hundreds of unauthorized refugees lived clandestinely in Moghilev.

Jagendorf was reluctant to become president of the Jewish Committee of Moghilev. He had no experience as a communal leader and felt vulnerable, telling Max Schmidt that he was "like a man in a glass booth, waiting for people to throw rocks." The composition of the Jewish Committee in Moghilev would change six times during the thirty-month exile. Jagendorf presided over the first three committees from November, 1941 to June, 1942, when he resigned for reasons that will be explained in a subsequent commentary.

*Part Two*

---

# WINTER, 1941–1942

FORCED LABOR

*Jagendorf Archives, Yad Vashem, The Holocaust Martyrs' and Heroes'
Remembrance Authority, Jerusalem*

The Jagendorf family flour mill, Zviniace, Bukovina, c. 1880 (*Courtesy of Adalbert Regenstreif*)

Siegfried Jagendorf (left) with fellow student at the Technikum Mittweida, Germany, 1904 (*Courtesy of Elfreda Stern and Edith Gitman*)

Wedding portrait, Siegfried and Hilda Jagendorf, Radautz, Bukovina, 1909 (*Courtesy of Elfreda Stern and Edith Gitman*)

Lieutenant Siegfried Jagendorf, Austrian Army, inducted into the order of Emperor Franz Josef, 1918 (*Courtesy of Elfreda Stern and Edith Gitman*)

Siegried Jagendorf (at the wheel), sister Mina (at his left), parents Abraham and Hannah Bassie (rear) and chauffeur Rudlev (front), Czernowitz, 1909 (*Courtesy of Elfreda Stern and Edith Gitman*)

Hilda Jagendorf with daughters Edith (left) and Elfreda, Czernowitz
(Cernauti), 1919 (*Courtesy of Elfreda Stern and Edith Gitman*)

Siegfried Jagendorf, director of Siemens–Schukert, Cernauti, c. 1922
(*Courtesy of Elfreda Stern and Edith Gitman*)

Dorohoi deportees prepare to cross the Dniester into Transnistria from Volcienetz, Bessarabia, June 10, 1942 (*Yad Vashem Archives, Jerusalem*)

Launching the barge at Volcienetz (*Yad Vashem Archives, Jerusalem*)

Orphan, Moghilev (*Jagendorf Archives, Yad Vashem, Jerusalem*)

Orphanage in Moghilev, c. 1943 (*Courtesy of Meir Shefi*)

Illustration of the Turnatoria by an unknown artist (*Jagendorf Archives, Yad Veshem, Jerusalem*)

Turnatoria lathe (*Jagendorf Archives, Yad Vashem, Jerusalem*)

Turnatoria workers end their shift (*Jagendorf Archives, Yad Vashem, Jerusalem*)

Max Schmidt surrounded by workers from the Turnatoria lathe and power plant department, 1943 (*Courtesy of Max Schmidt*)

Dr. Wilhelm Filderman (seated center) with Siegfried Jagendorf (front left), Moses Katz (front right). Standing (left to right) Max Schmidt, Max Heissman, "Baby" David, unidentified, and Pinkas Katz. Moghilev, 1943 (*Courtesy of Ion Butnaru*)

Cigarette lighters produced in the Turnatoria: the one on the left is inscribed with Jagendorf's signature, the other bears the initials E G, for Edith Gitman

PREFECTURA *Jud. Moghilev*

## PERMIS de CONDUCERE
### PENTRU
# AUTOMOBILE

Nr. *9029* din *2 Septembrie* 194*2*

D-l *Ing. Siegfried Jaegendorf*

Profesiunea *Director al Turnatoriei*
*lui Moghilev*

Nationalitatea _____

Domiciliat *Moghilev*
*Str. Traiana 5*

nascut in anul 194_ luna *August* ziua *1*
admis a conduce auto-vehicolele de orice
categorie, comform art. 9 din ordonanta № 75
a Guvernamantului Transnistriei, a primit
acest permis de conducere.

*Moghilev 2 Septembrie* 194*2*

PREFECT *[signature]*

atura titularului _____
*[signature]*

Driver's license issued to Turnatoria director Siegfried Jagendorf by the Prefecture of Moghilev, September 2, 1942 (*Jagendorf Archives, Yad Vashem, Jerusalem*)

Jagendorf, Turnatoria, c. 1943 (*Jagendorf Archives, Yad Vashem, Jerusalem*)

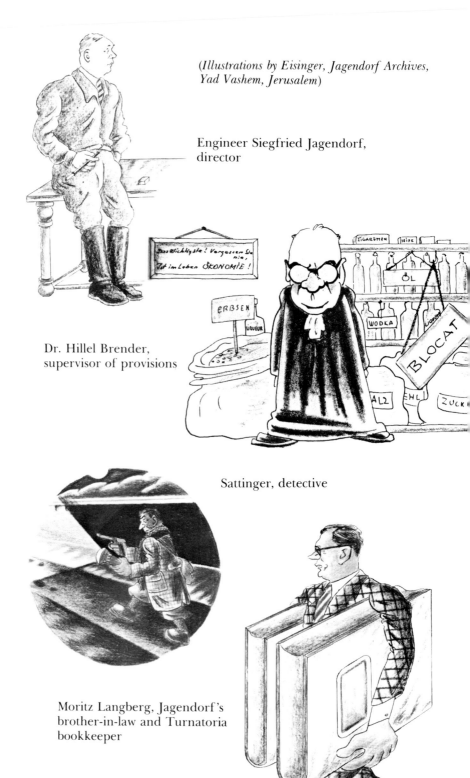

(*Illustrations by Eisinger, Jagendorf Archives, Yad Vashem, Jerusalem*)

Engineer Siegfried Jagendorf, director

Dr. Hillel Brender, supervisor of provisions

Sattinger, detective

Moritz Langberg, Jagendorf's brother-in-law and Turnatoria bookkeeper

Pinkus Katz, superintendent

Samuel Kurzweill, architect and
designer of monumental crucifix

Engineer Max Schmidt, deputy
superintendent and director of lathe
and power department

Stenographer Brüll

One-way travel certificate allows the Jagendorfs to exit Romania but not to return, May 20, 1946 (*Courtesy of Elfreda Stern and Edith Gitman*)

MR. AND MRS. SIEGFRIED JAEGENDORF

The Dayton Journal's January 2, 1947 edition reports on the reunification of the Jagendorf family.

# Parents, Persecuted By Hitler, Arrive Here To Visit Daughter

**By JAMES NICHOLS**

The dreams of more than eight years came true for Mr. and Mrs. Siegfried Jaegendorf, late of Botoshanie, Romania, yesterday when they arrived in Dayton to visit their daughters, Mrs. William Gitman of 1108 Salem avenue.

During those eight years since the couple had last seen their daughter they had known all the fury of Hitler's fanaticism against the Jewish race. Jaegendorf had risen above the "mortal storm" to become the outstanding leader of the Jewish people in Romania. But those terrible days seem far away now as they renew acquaintances with their daughter, their son-in-law, Dr. William Gitman and meet the Gitman twins, Stuart Steven and Alan Howard, 2.

Part of their dream had come true Christmas Day when their plane settled down at LaGuardia field, New York and they were re-united with their other daughter, Mrs. Henry Stern. They will return to New York after a visit to take up permanent residence.

Mrs. Jaegendorf, a small shy woman, speaks no English at all and her husband speaks very little. But he told the story of his war years with Dr. Gitman as an interpreter.

The Jaegendorfs first ran afoul of Hitler in March, 1938, when Nazi troops marched into Vienna. Three days later the Jaegendorfs left their home in Vienna and returned to Cernouti in the province of Boucovena in Romania. Shortly thereafter, Jaegendorf, an electrical engineer and reserve officer, was called into the Romanian army where he served until the end of 1940.

Once Antonescu and Hitler gained control of Romania in 1941, Jaegendorf knew that bad days were ahead for him and his people. Soon the Nazi horde struck, moving all Jews from the villages, stripping them of all their possessions and forcing them to wander.

They were forced to march as the German army pushed back the Russian force. At one time they were dying at the rate of 100 a day. Finally they arrived at the Ukrainian city of Mogolav and for some 80,000 the wandering was over.

The Germans called for Jaegendorf to organize and rehabilitate the town for their troops. He accepted after the Germans agreed that he could use his people to do the work.

It wasn't until March, 1944 that the Russian spearhead pushing out from Stalingrad freed them. During that time they had managed to live and fight back at Nazis. After being liberated the Jaegendorfs returned to Romania.

But the fight was not over for the husband. When the war ended he became one of the chief witnesses for the Romanian government in the trying of Romanian war criminals.

Siegfried "Sam" Jagendorf, Southern California, 1955 (*Courtesy of Ann H. Stern*)

# 1

## FORCED LABOR

The mass infiltration of Jews from the camps back to Moghilev worried me. As a defensive measure I wrote a memorandum alerting the city's police chief. Shortly thereafter, we received the following notification: "Within four days all the Jews in Moghilev without authorization will present themselves at the police station. After this date the police will conduct raids and arrest all Jews failing to report. They will be treated as spies, shot where they are caught."

The authorities held the Jewish Committee responsible but refrained from punishing us because we could prove that we had called for preventive action. Having blunted the attack on the Jewish leadership, we could provide the "illegals" with authorizations taken from the deceased. And we secured the release of jailed Jews by adding their names to the labor rolls. Every day the Germans demanded additional Jewish workers be sent across the Bug River. Observing the number of Jews loitering on the streets of Moghilev, the Germans accused the Romanians of squandering a valuable strategic resource. Delivering Jews to the Germans beyond the Bug River meant handing them to the executioner, I therefore considered it my paramount task to persuade the Romanians that no authorized

Jewish worker could be spared. At the same time, I had to convince the Jews that only by productive work could they be saved. But many Jews preferred to engage in black market activities, arousing the displeasure of the authorities who had issued them authorizations on my assurance that their labor was indispensable. Delinquent workers compromised my credibility and endangered us all.

The situation became so serious that the Romanian officials threatened to hand the Germans any Jews who were found absent from their assigned work stations. At that point, I advised the committee to create an office for the coordination of Jewish labor. Men between the ages of 18 and 55 had to register and be prepared to work every day of the week. Those declared physically unfit by our doctors received exemptions. Jewish supervisors commanded units of thirty men. To obtain workers for a given job, the authorities were asked to file a written report with the prefect twenty-four hours in advance, indicating the number of workers needed and the type of work. This procedure often broke down because certain military units made sport of dragooning Jews off the streets and wanted no part of lists that showed how many "Yids" were taken and how many returned.

Our security depended to a large extent on the official relationships we had cultivated, so the dismissal of the gendarme commander, Major Danulescu, for aiding Jews came as a great blow. A member of our community, Judge Simon Hilsenrad, had received a repatriation order to Radauti. Major Danulescu agreed to assign as escorts two sympathetic policemen who permitted Judge Hilsenrad to arrange a shipment of food and clothing to us. The Romanian secret service foiled the plan. Judge Hilsenrad and the policemen were arrested and a highly publicized trial followed. The policemen received long prison terms and the judge was returned to Moghilev. Major Danulescu lost his command but after the war was exonerated by a military tribunal on the basis of our testimony.

# 2

# THE BEATING

I FOLLOWED A regular daily routine: in the factory from 7:00
A.M. until noon, followed by a half-mile walk to the Jewish Committee office in the municipal building. Shortly after leaving the
Turnatoria on the afternoon of January 20, 1942, someone
called to me from the military barracks. I turned and recognized Engineer Kamilo Kaufman. Entering the building, I saw
about one hundred Jewish men in the yard standing in formation before a Romanian officer and several armed soldiers. I
approached the officer and said, "My name is Engineer Siegfried Jagendorf. I am in charge of worker recruitment here.
You have no right to detain these people. If you need laborers,
you must request them in writing from the prefect."

"Who the hell are you," the officer yelled, hitting me in the
face. In an instant the soldiers set upon me and Engineer
Kaufman, hammering us with their rifle butts. Then they emptied our pockets and shoved us in a tiny jail cell to await the
firing squad. Every few minutes a guard would swing open the
heavy door and whack us with a wooden plank. Blood covered
my clothes.

After an hour, soldiers took Engineer Kaufman. I heard
voices in the yard but no shots. Another hour passed. Finally a

Romanian lieutenant entered the cell and escorted me to his office. He apologized for the incident and informed me that we were expected at police headquarters, where proper action would be taken. He excused himself and gave the guards strict orders not to touch me. The lieutenant returned with the guilty officer, Aurel Popescu, and the three of us left the barracks under heavy guard.

I assumed they had discovered from my confiscated papers that, as head of the Jewish Committee, I had been within my rights. The police chief, a major, apologized for the "unfortunate occurence." Beating a Jew, it should be understood, was standard operating procedure in Transnistria, never censured or punished. Nevertheless, the major berated my attacker for his cowardly conduct: "You are no hero, beating a defenseless man. What can I expect from someone lacking education and common sense? You are unworthy of your uniform. In your entire life, you have not done for Romania what this man has in the short time he's been here." The police chief reiterated his regrets and sent me home with an escort. Popescu lost his furlough and was promptly recalled to the front. I remained in bed for the next three weeks, suffering from internal injuries and a throat wound that required surgery. My life, I learned later, had been saved by the prefect. He had phoned the military barracks after being alerted by my secretary.

On the morning of February 12, 1942, I returned to the Turnatoria. At the entrance, the commander of the Romanian regiment accosted me and said, "Mr. Engineer, I presume you have arranged for the 800 workers I will need tomorrow morning."

"This is the first I've heard of it," I complained. "We are just now reorganizing our labor office and cannot possibly comply with your request."

"I have orders from the general to shoot you on the spot if you do not fulfill your obligation by tomorrow morning at seven. And I shall be there personally to count them."

I asked the prefect to block the order or, at least, to send off the workers with food. Colonel Baleanu approved the rations.

I returned to my office with little hope of recruiting even a fraction of the 800 men. I summoned Mihail Danilof, head of our labor coordinating office, and asked him to assemble some workers as a gesture of compliance. He told me that the effort already was under way.

Still very sick, I rose early the next morning and walked to the assembly place in front of the prefectura. Jews streamed in from all sides and formed columns. At precisely 7:00 A.M., the colonel, flanked by a firing squad, greeted me courteously. Then he faced the columns and counted. Completing his tally, the colonel said, "Good work, Mr. Engineer, we have more than 1,000 men." I was dumbfounded. The volunteers included doctors, judges, and lawyers—categories exempted from hard labor.

When the laborers returned three days later, many of them suffering from severe frostbite, I asked one of them why so many people willingly had placed their lives at risk to save me. He replied, "What would happen to us without you? We came forward not only to save your life, but our own."

# 3

# A RIGHTEOUS
# ROMANIAN

Despite all our efforts, the Turnatoria generated no income, leaving us extremely vulnerable. The Germans could have demanded the closing of the factory and ordered us all shot for perpetrating a hoax. We needed an initial sale, but to whom? Transnistria was a military zone closed to unauthorized civilians.

Deliverance came in the person of Ion Larionescu, a wealthy Radauti horsebreeder whom I had known for many years. He arrived in Moghilev on a business permit but actually was secreting money to his deported friends. This righteous man had served coincidentally as a fellow officer with Colonel Baleanu in the first world war. I saw in Mr. Larionescu's arrival an act of providence and intended to exploit the opportunity fully.

I proposed privately that Mr. Larionescu ask the prefect for an export permit to ship a quantity of stoves to Romania. "The prefect," I explained, "will ask me if the Turnatoria had the capacity to fill the order. I will say yes and give him the price per unit. Then you will offer Colonel Baleanu a sum greater than my figure, sign the contract, and pay in advance. I will repay you later." Mr. Larionescu readily agreed to the scheme and told me not to worry about the money. The cash in the prefect's hand gave substance to what had until now been a vague promise, enhancing our status beyond measure.

Mr. Larionescu did not demand delivery of the stoves, allowing us to install them in our unheated hospitals and home for the elderly. Unfortunately, on a subsequent mercy mission to Transnistria our courageous Romanian ally was caught and sentenced to ten years at hard labor.

# 4

# INFORMERS

Jews who had made private deals with various Romanian officials considered themselves untouchable, forgetting that personal gain, not altruism, motivated our adversaries. When the deal no longer suited the official, the Jew was left without protection and often thrown in jail or worse. In such cases, I sided with the Romanians, upon whose future cooperation I depended. Later, I would arrange the release of the Jew, promising the police that we would discipline him, and we did. In this manner we saved the culprit's life and contained scandals that might have resulted in collective punishment.

Many workers thought me unduly severe and autocratic, faulting me for punishing those who broke the rules or produced items in the factory for exchange on the black market. The Turnatoria could shield us only so long as we kept ourselves perfectly clean. We had to reinforce constantly the perception among the Germans and Romanians that we worked for them, not for ourselves. The slightest suspicion that Jews were profiting from the enterprises we managed could have resulted in our demise; therefore, it was essential that each of us comply with all rules and regulations. As the person responsible for the security and survival of the community, it was my task to demand and to ensure that our people acted correctly at all times.

The Turnatoria was under the surveillance of informers, Jews enlisted by various Romanian officials to uncover irregularities in our operations. Like the other workers, however, these spies were kept totally in the dark about the policy decisions made by me in consultation with my inner circle—Dr. Jonas Kessler, Dr. Hillel Brender, Mr. Max Heissman, Mr. David Rennert, and Mr. Pinkas Katz.

Neutralization of Jewish informers began shortly after they entered the factory. I told them privately that, given the circumstances, I did not blame them for the betrayal. Then I proposed to help them work up their weekly reports by providing detailed information that would make them look good to their masters but cause us no harm. I promised that our collaboration would remain top secret. Though initially reluctant to cooperate, the informers soon realized that they could learn nothing of significance without my assistance. Furthermore, these uneducated people could not write a lucid intelligence report, even if they had the information. So we wrote the reports, giving detailed accounts of my callous disregard for the well-being of the workers, especially the sick and starving. This charade convinced the authorities of my loyalty.

# 5

## TYPHUS

TYPHUS BROKE out in December, 1941. Hundreds of Jews died each day from this endemic lice-borne disease. We had to double the number of gravediggers. Eight of our seventy doctors died attempting to heal the sick without medicine, disinfectant, or soap. Entire families were wiped out. Typhus posed a secondary threat as well; fearing a wider outbreak of the epidemic that might infect the military, the authorities could easily have chosen to exterminate us rather than the lice.

To enforce cleanliness, we secretly produced soap and constructed a communal bath house that was heated by a diesel-powered furnace made in the Turnatoria. Every member of the factory community was required to take a weekly bath according to a strict timetable. Anyone failing to bathe without a legitimate excuse was reported to me and punished. Our medical personnel examined each person for cleanliness and for evidence of lice. Anyone found to have typhus was transferred immediately to our hospital for contagious diseases. The daily report delivered to my desk at 7:00 A.M. listed the names of persons who neglected the sanitary rules, carried lice, or contracted typhus. The first time a person was found to be infested with lice, he received a written warning; the second time his food ration was cut; the third time he was expelled from the Turnatoria community, resulting in the loss of his authorization and all that went with it—bread, a roof, soap, hot water, and medicine. Still, some people abused these privileges and paid dearly.

One day in March, 1942, all the Jewish doctors and I were called to a meeting in the office of Major Dr. C. Chirila. The Romanian medical officer opened the session with a stinging attack on our doctors, accusing them of negligence in failing to control the plague. The physicians protested that they had no disinfectants, no drugs. Dr. Chirila scolded the doctors for making excuses and threatened them with severe punishment should they fail to implement his sanitation program. Before dismissing us, he promised to supply the necessary hygienic and pharmaceutical supplies.

Dr. Chirila asked me to remain behind after the meeting. When we were alone, he handed me a package of letters from Bucharest. "I have come here to help you," he said. "Let me know if you would like me to take anything back to the capital." Fearing a trap, I told him that such things take time and asked if we could meet again. He told me where to reach him and we parted with a handshake.

I rejoined the Jewish doctors outside. They likened Dr. Chirila to Hitler and asked me what would become of us. I dared not reveal the medical officer's noble intentions, certainly not with so many informers around. I advised them to do their part and let me handle the rest. My investigation of Dr. Chirila revealed that he was the top-ranking hospital official in Bucharest whose father-in-law had been assassinated by the Iron Guard. The influential Dr. Chirila proved to be a valuable ally.

About that time, I received a letter from Bukovina inquiring about the fate of two women who had been deported to Transnistria. They were the wife and eighteen-year-old daughter of Dr. Albert Pilpel, a famous Jewish chemist whose expertise kept him in Cernauti, where he worked in a sugar manufacturing plant. It usually took me about a month to locate someone in one of the Lager; more often than not, I learned that the person had died. In this case, I located the two women and asked the camp's Jewish chief to visit me in Moghilev. When Mr. Rosenberg arrived, he informed me about the pitiful state of the two women and agreed to take them some money and clothes. A week later, Mr. Rosenberg brought me the following letter from the daughter, Gertrude Pilpel:

"Although I do not know you, I wish to thank you for the 50 marks you sent me by way of Mr. Rosenberg. I am sorry to say that it arrived too late. My mother died at noon today. Now, at nineteen, I remain alone. I also received the dress, blouse, and two shirts from Mrs. Jagendorf, for which I am very thankful. I had nothing to wear. I still need a skirt, a warm jacket, a pair of shoes, size 38 (mine are completely torn apart), a pair of stockings, two handkerchiefs, a comb, and soap."

We sent her what we could, knowing that a single girl without protection was doomed. Mr. Rosenberg told me that the girl's body was covered with lice and scabies. She was a perfect candidate for typhus. Mrs. Jagendorf decided the girl should be brought to Moghilev and live with us.

I asked Mr. Rosenberg to look after Miss Pilpel until she was fit to travel. Several weeks later, he reported that his charge was ready. Gertrude stayed with us for months, until Dr. Pilpel convinced the government to repatriate her to Cernauti.

The winter of 1941–1942 brought unspeakable suffering to the Jews beyond the Dniester. Neither the Romanian government nor the Jewish Center in Bucharest responded to our urgent appeals for food, fuel, medicine, and other vital supplies.

At the request of the Nazis, the Romanian government established the Jewish Center (Central Office of the Jews) in February, 1942, replacing Dr. Wilhelm Filderman's Union of Jewish Communities. We sent the following appeal to the Jewish Center two weeks after its formation:

"Our census of last month showed 12,500 deported Jews in the city of Moghilev. There are undoubtedly more; many people have returned here secretly from the camps. We assume that we presently have 15,000 Jews. Unauthorized Jews have caused us a great deal of trouble. The authorities have ordered them to surrender by tomorrow night, and we do not know what awaits them.

"We serve a warm meal to 4,500–5,000 persons daily in our communal soup kitchen, which is the only food they receive. In an Orthodox canteen under the supervision of Rabbis Ginsberg and Derbarmdiker another 1,000 persons receive a daily portion. Two hundred orphans are fed at another pantry, and fifty of them receive shelter. Our soup kitchens cannot satisfy the growing demand.

"We run an old-age home for 250 people. Our hospital for contagious diseases has 100 patients, two per bed. Another 80-bed hospital accommodates 120 patients. All our efforts notwithstanding, typhus is spreading out of control; not a single household is without at least one infected person. Our good friend Mr. Feiwel Laufer and Drs. Gottlieb and Weissmann are among the victims. Six doctors are critically ill.

"In the past two weeks we have had to buy medicine at black market prices. How the profiteers obtain this precious commodity, while we cannot, remains a mystery. We are well aware that all of us are destined to die in this place, but we will not stop working even for a minute to save at least a part of our youth.

"You cannot imagine how bad things are elsewhere in the district [of Moghilev]. There are no words to describe what we hear from these naked and starving people. We can offer them only an occasional loaf of bread.

"The daily cost of running the soup kitchen in this city is 100,000 lei [$500]; the hospitals require another 50,000 lei [$250]. What little transportation we have managed to procure adds another 10,000 lei [$50] to our daily outlay. Fuel is unattainable at any price. Soap and disinfectants are priced beyond our reach.

"Despite all this misery, our people are willing to work, if given a chance. Yesterday we could not prevent the evacuation of 1,000 Jews from the city.

"Our bookkeeping department will send you a balance sheet in the next few days. You may ask what is the source of our funds. Those who arrived with some money made loans to the committee. If we are unable to repay them, they too will starve.

"For your information, we are recording one hundred deaths per day, keeping thirty gravediggers busy. Still, the corpses are piling up. Many of these deaths were preventable. . . .

"Gentlemen, you have our report. If we do not receive in the next days a massive shipment of money, medicine, etc., we will be compelled to close all our institutions, resign from the committee, and leave all in chaos and disaster. The responsibility would be yours. Should the reason for your unwillingness to help be that you distrust us, appoint your own people, and we will give them our full support."

We had no intention of actually leaving all in a state of chaos. We upgraded our living quarters both at the school and nearby annexes by adding a communal bakery, pantry, laundry, and school. Undernourished children were given a supplementary diet, including milk. Workers received one daily meal of soup and bread in the Turnatoria kitchen.

All food and other necessities were divided without discrimination. Each one of us, including me, received the same ration.

# 6

# "LAUNDERING" LEI

DESPITE OUR appeals to the Jewish Center, almost no money reached us during the terrible winter months. The Jewish leadership in Bucharest was not to blame. Funds sent from Bucharest had to be converted to RKKS marks and transferred to us via the Romanian National Bank. The Germans set the exchange rate at sixty lei to one RKKS mark, six times the rate available on the open market. As a result, we would receive only a fraction of the financial assistance, and only after long delays deliberately imposed by the authorities. In Transnistria Jews were forbidden to possess lei under penalty of death.

This situation forced us to run underground couriers, drawing primarily upon Romanian, German, and Italian military personnel. They were paid dearly for delivering money and valuables from Romanian Jewish sources to the exiles in Transnistria. The couriers frequently pocketed the aid, claiming it had been confiscated at a military or gendarme checkpoint. That was a lie; anyone caught smuggling aid to Jews was arrested and sentenced by the military court to a long prison term.

The Turnatoria bookkeeper exchanged the lei for RKKS marks on the black market and entered the sums in our books as factory earnings. The Jewish Committee in Moghilev "laundered" lei by crediting the funds as income from the cemetery department. During the first winter, when our death rate approached one hundred per day, the cemetery department director compiled lists of those who had died heirless. We then recorded the lei in our books as RKKS marks recovered from the pockets of the deceased. Thus we kept our books in balance and stretched our funds for the benefit of the colony's welfare institutions.

We also finessed the rules regarding bread rations. Ordinance No. 23 entitled only employed Jews to receive one pound of bread per day; nothing was provided for family members. We interpreted the ordinance to allow a daily bread ration for all workers' dependents—an interpretation that went unchallenged for the duration.

# 7

## JEWISH POLICE

THE AUTHORITIES granted my request for the formation of a Jewish police force to guard our institutions. While thinking about a suitable candidate for chief, I received the following letter from Pauline Kapise in the Sargorod Lager:

"Based on our short acquaintance, I am allowing myself, without the knowledge of my husband, to ask for your help. We are in the greatest need. For months my husband and I and our only child have been starving. We cannot expect any help from our friends in Romania because we have no way to contact them. Please, Mr. Engineer, help us if you can. You are our last resort. Do not let us die, and consider our child."

Letters of desperation reached me daily from the camps, but the simple plea of Pauline Kapise impressed me. Alfred Kapise had been an attorney and a Romanian reserve officer. When I met him briefly in Moghilev, he struck me as an upstanding and dignified man. I decided he would make an ideal police chief and requested that the prefect issue him and his family authorizations to stay in Moghilev. Colonel Baleanu's reaction was predictable: "How can you ask me to bring in more Jews, when we have far too many already? Can't you find a chief among the thousands of refugees already here?"

"No, I cannot, Mr. Prefect, because the people who are authorized to stay are specialists. This job requires a man who is beyond any hint of corruption. Don't you see how the mentality of our people has changed? Everyone thinks only of himself and his children; he acts without the slightest consideration for the well-being of others. He will steal, do anything to preserve himself and his kin. I need a chief who can bring these base impulses under control and still conduct himself in a decent and correct manner. It is in your best interest, Mr. Prefect, to have a man like Kapise here to enforce law and order."

Colonel Baleanu signed the authorization, and a few days later Alfred and Pauline Kapise arrived in Moghilev with their eight-year-old daughter. I told Mr. Kapise that he would receive a sufficient salary to cover his family's basic needs. In order to stamp out the black marketeers and others who thrived shamelessly on despair and misfortune, Kapise would have to remain financially independent. No one else received wages.

We entrusted to Mr. Kapise the running of our intelligence gathering operation. Until that time, our informers—attorneys and other professionals who worked as clerks and typists in various government offices—often had failed to give us advance warning of impending anti-Jewish measures. I relied on Mr. Kapise to find a way of infiltrating the higher echelons.

Meanwhile, repair of the machinery inside the Turnatoria proceeded at a perilous pace. I feared that the Germans and Romanians might lose interest in our enterprise and in us. The credibility we had garnered by restoring electric power and the stove deal no longer sufficed; we needed a new triumph.

But how could we impress them with our technical proficiency, when every factory tool had to be produced laboriously by hand? I wondered what had happened to the implements. Did the Russians who had abandoned valuable raw materials have time to gather and pack tools? Not likely. Former factory workers must have pilfered them. I didn't want to alienate the local population by reporting the theft to the authorities, so I met with several trustworthy Ukrainian Turnatoria hands and asked for their help. I pointed out that we were allies in the struggle against Hitler and that the Turnatoria would benefit us all. I also promised to pay cash. Within days, many of the missing tools reappeared, allowing us to accelerate the repair of the machines.

*Commentary for Part Two*

---

# Winter, 1941–1942

THE UNITED STATES entered the war against Japan one day after the December 7, 1941 attack on Pearl Harbor. Germany and Italy responded by declaring war on the United States. On the eastern front, the Soviets launched a counteroffensive from Moscow in early December and within weeks contained the Axis advance. Hitler's army had lost nearly one million men, thousands of tanks, planes, trucks, and artillery pieces. The Reich also lost its air of invincibility.

Germany's war against the Jews suffered no such setbacks. The Einsatzgruppen continued their genocidal operations in the occupied zones of the Soviet Union. Meanwhile, Nazi technicians experimented with poison gas and readied a network of killing centers for the "special treatment" of the continent's entire Jewish population. On January 20, 1942, at Wannsee, near Berlin, representatives of Germany's ministries learned from Reinhard Heydrich, head of the Reich Security Main Office (RSHA), exactly how Germany planned to implement the "final solution" to the Jewish problem. Nazi demographers had calculated that another eleven million Jews remained in Europe, including 342,000 in Romania and 2,994,684 in the Ukraine.

---

The Antonescu regime dissolved the Union of Jewish Communities in December, 1941, replacing it later with the Jewish Center (Centrala Evreilor in Romanian, Juden Centrale in German). The Jewish Center was headed nominally by Dr. Nandor Gingold, a Jewish physician who had converted to Christianity. He took his orders from the Romanian government's commissar for Jewish affairs, Radu Lecca, who maintained close contact with Adolf Eichmann's aide in Bucharest, SS Haupsturmfuehrer Gustav Richter. The Jewish Center collected government-imposed "contributions" of money and property from Romanian Jews, supplied forced labor battalions, and compiled names and addresses of Jews in preparation for the "final solution" of Romania's Jewish problem, mass deportation to the Nazi extermination camp at Belzec. Romania's postwar People's Court convicted Nandor Gingold as a major war criminal. After serving a long prison term, he tried unsuccessfully to clear his name, claiming he had aided the deported Jews in Transnistria. Gingold died in Bucharest in 1989.

---

The typhus epidemic (more accurately a pandemic that included a number of infectious diseases including typhoid fever, typhus exanthematic, and tuberculosis) struck Moghilev in December, 1941. Of the approximately 7,000 Jews infected, fewer than half recovered. In Bersad, the alternate destination of the Radauti transports, an estimated 20,000 Jews perished in the plague.

One survivor told me that his strongest image of Moghilev was that of typhus victims stacked in a horse-drawn cart, their legs vibrating over the edge as the vehicle crawled toward the graveyard.

These deaths could have been prevented had the Romanian authorities not restricted the flow of aid to the ghettos and camps in Transnistria. Moreover, the legion of gendarmes in Moghilev stepped up surveillance along the Dniester, confiscating money, food, and medicine.

In the Turnatoria, engineer Max Schmidt avoided wearing a coat in freezing temperatures in dread of lice lodging in the layers of his clothing. He recalls:

"My department was in wretched shape, cold and full of draughts. The starving, shivering workers grouped around little fires on the factory floor to keep warm. Fearing that a louse could easily spread the infection by passing from one person to the next, I lectured a group of young men about the dangers of such close contact. The next day I was informed that one of the youths in my department who earlier had been infected died that morning from typhoid fever. The loss so shocked me that I decided to be ruthless in preventing workers from huddling together."

Deprived of medical instruments and supplies, Jewish doctors could do little more than quarantine the victims. In Moghilev and Sargorod, twenty-three doctors died in their futile attempt to contain the plague. At the end of April, 1942, a top official of the health ministry, Major Dr. C. Chirila, provided medicines that halted the five-month pestilence in ten days.

Deportees bartered their last possessions to obtain medicines for their stricken loved ones. Mark Brandman, whose family was deported from Gura–Humora in southern Bukovina to Murafa, one of the 67 Lager in the Moghilev district, described to me how he had saved his brother:

"One night my fifteen-year-old brother and three of his friends contracted typhus while playing cards; a louse jumped from one onto the other. Complications from the disease caused my brother's head to swell up and fill with pus. When the doctor told me that there was no hope of recovery, I refused to accept his opinion and told him I would get the necessary medicine. He looked at me as if I were crazy and told me that he needed surgical instruments. I persuaded him to provide me with a detailed list. Then, without asking my mother, I removed her precious Persian lamb coat from its hiding place and offered it to the furrier. He said he could cut it up and make hats that would dazzle the Ukrainians. We struck a deal and he agreed to advance me some of the money. I sought the help of a young Jewish woman, who was the lover of the local Romanian military commander. She agreed to ask the commander to recommend a trustworthy officer who would accept a generous commission to bring the medical supplies from Bucharest to Murafa. I paid the officer, he delivered the goods, and the doctor performed the surgery on our kitchen table. The coat could not have been put to better use. My brother now lives in New York. His face still bears the scars."

The Jewish leadership in Bucharest could do little to soften the blow dealt the deportees in Transnistria during the record cold winter of 1941. One Moghilev survivor remarked, "Your spit would freeze before hitting the ground." Another commented, "You almost could see the shape of your words as they left your mouth."

Of an estimated 150,000 Romanian Jews exiled to Transnistria, about half perished during the first year, most of them from deprivation of food, medicine, and fuel. In contrast to the more disciplined German mass murderers, the Romanians generally did not approach the task systematically and were readily swayed by gifts and other favors. These weaknesses allowed adroit and energetic Jewish leaders such as Siegfried Jagendorf to undermine the extermination effort.

The following report signed by Major D. Iliescu of the Inspectorate of Gendarmes in Chisinau (Kish-in-oh), dated January 3, 1941, gives a Romanian perspective on the state of affairs in Moghilev during the first winter of the exile:

"Close to 2,000–5,000 deported Jews from Bukovina remain in Moghilev; some carry on business, some have opened trade shops, others work in the fittings factory in that locality.

"The Jews of Moghilev and those from other localities east of Moghilev are contacting the Jews of Bucharest through Christian intermediaries who clandestinely bring hundreds of letters from one part to another. In the past five or six days alone, three individuals carrying 215 letters from Transnistria to Jewish institutions in Bucharest have been apprehended. In the other direction, letters, various objects, and money are sent to Transnistria. When they cannot enter Transnistria due to the vigilance of the gendarmes and customs agents, they operate through the military in Moghilev, avoiding our controls. . . .

"The iron works in Moghilev is full of Jews, from the director and assistant down.

"The letters . . . are written mostly in the German language. From reading the few letters in Romanian, we can state that the Jews complain about the misery and lack of necessities. . . .

"They [the Jews] deal in all kinds of contraband, especially in matches, which . . . bring 20 lei [ten cents] per box.

"The Romanian element is in control but corrupted by the Jewish element. Two Jewesses work at the officers' canteen, five Jews are employed at the prefecture, and officers have Jewish mistresses. . . . The Jewish element has excellent relations with the military and civil authorities, from the prefecture to the police. The Jewess Carmen Dickmann and her friend Hilde have ingratiated themselves with the authorities. I am told that both attend soirées . . . amusing themselves greatly in the company of officers and civil servants. At one party, Carmen Dickmann ridiculed the Ukrainian women for their dresses and manners, stressing that they do not know how to hold their handkerchiefs. . . .

"Two [gendarme] agents were sent to Moghilev to make contact with the Jews and offer themselves as couriers. They received fifteen letters addressed to Cernauti, where the Jewish recipients gave them 22,500 lei [$112.50] and the attached letters. . . .

"The Ukrainian population is agitated and displeased with the state of affairs in Moghilev—the special, favorable treatment of Jews . . . who find the means to buy everything at inflated prices. The Jewess Carmen Dickmann has stated that the Ukrainians hate the Jews to such an extent that if Moghilev for any reason were without an army, all the Jews would be massacred. . . ."

The Jewish Committee of Moghilev attempted without much success to rein in Jews who aroused suspicion among the authorities. On December 11, 1941, Jagendorf issued the following warning:

"The Romanian military and civil authorities have notified us that deported Jews holding authorizations to remain in Moghilev do not honor their obligation inasmuch as they do not show up for work regularly. Therefore, the Romanian authorities will begin to punish delinquent workers by revoking their authorizations. Able-bodied workers have been congregating on the streets during job hours. . . . Should the authorities arrest delinquent workers, do not expect the committee to intervene. You must understand that the committee defends only the disciplined workers who do their jobs."

In response to the growing number of unauthorized Jews migrating back to Moghilev from outlying camps, Jagendorf declared:

"No person is permitted to give shelter to those infiltrating from the camps. You are obliged to inform the police if you know the whereabouts of such illegal persons. The police have orders to apprehend these persons and turn them in to the gendarmes. Anyone found sheltering such persons will be severely punished. The supervisor for each street section will investigate whether such people are hiding in their area. We ask the Jewish population to pay attention to this order because of the serious consequences."

To enforce the Jewish Committee's directives pertaining to worker discipline and to supply the authorities with laborers in an orderly and equitable manner, Jagendorf created the Office for the Coordination of Jewish Labor. He also established the ghetto police to uphold forced labor conscription and to maintain law and order. These measures, meant to enhance communal security, led to flagrant abuses of power and corruption, resulting in Jewish resentment against the committee.

In February, 1942, an internal investigation of Moghilev's Jewish police, ordered by Jagendorf, disclosed fundamental problems. The report noted that the police force functioned inadequately because it was obliged to serve the dictates of both Romanian and Jewish authorities. Moreover, its blatant absence of discipline impeded its ability to oversee forced labor, control illicit trade and the flow of contraband, enforce tax collection, apprehend fugitives, and perform routine police work. "The force requires upstanding people," the report concluded, "but honesty and normality are tied to minimal existence. Therefore, to prevent corruption and graft, the police should receive a minimum salary. Until this is done, the police will not attract the right element. . . . The police of today has become an organization of power and an instrument of different political factions in the service of known political figures."

In his recent book on Transnistria, *Burning Ice: The Ghettos of Transnistria* (Hebrew), Dr. Avigdor Shachan maintained that the Jewish police in Moghilev exceeded all other camps and ghettos in cruelty toward fellow Jews, and that the Jewish Committee was aware of these abuses but chose to ignore the complaints and refused to remove the offenders. He cites two examples of how the ghetto police dealt with Jews who had escaped to Moghilev from other camps. In the first, Lea Klarstein recalled: "Jewish policemen tracked down Jews who had escaped from the other side of the Bug River and threatened to expose them unless they paid hush money." In the second incident, a witness testified: "One day a police officer, the right-hand man of a (Jewish) committee member who directed the police, confronted the family that protected me. He demanded that I accompany him to the police station. Everyone pleaded with him to leave me alone. He said if I don't come immediately, he would have his dog tear me to pieces. I followed the policeman to see the committee member, who shouted at me, beat me, and ripped my only shirt. Afterwards, I was dragged by the police to the railroad station and deported with others to Peciora on the Bug River."

Turnatoria workers carried authorizations exempting them from interference by the Jewish labor coordinating office. At times, however, Mihail Danilof's enforcers would ignore the special status of the factory workers, forcing them to clear rubble, unload vehicles, or engage in other forms of exhausting labor. Such encroachments infuriated Jagendorf, who, according to Max Schmidt, would assail Danilof and threaten, "Take me, but keep away from my workers."

In April, 1943, Danilof responded defiantly to Jagendorf's complaint about the arrest of sixteen Dorohoi Jews: "For your information, I consider myself a partner of yours and no way subservient to you. . . ." Danilof pointed out that, as the one responsible for coordinating labor, he had the most difficult function, one that had turned the people against him. He said, "I execute this task as a moral responsibility . . . and I will not take orders from you. No! Never! If you do not agree, then I will resign."

---

Jagendorf recounts how Ion Larionescu, a wealthy Radauti horse breeder, invested the Turnatoria with credibility by paying the prefect for stoves that he knew would never be delivered. Larionescu's "crime" of aiding the deportees was cited in a police report, dated January 3, 1942, which also noted the activities of Albert Twers, a lawyer of German ethnic origin who was apprehended at a railroad station "with 139 letters written by deported Jews to those remaining in the country, particularly in Cernauti and Radauti." The report stated that the investigation of Albert Twers "did not establish that he received money but affirmed that this way of correspondence, practiced on a grand scale, contravenes postal and censorship laws."

The interventions of a small number of courageous non-Jews who opposed Antonescu's anti-Semitic policies contributed significantly to the redemption of the exiles in Transnistria. One of the outstanding "righteous gentiles" during the Romanian Holocaust was Traian Popovici, who, while mayor of Cernauti, delayed the deportation of thousands of the city's Jews by issuing them exemptions. The mayor was dismissed for his pro-Jewish sympathies, and Jews holding "Popovici papers" were put on trains to Transnistria in the summer of 1942.

Dr. Pepi Summer, a child survivor of Transnistria who currently lives in Buffalo, New York, recounted what happened when her family's Popovici exemption lost its protective power:

"Late one night, policemen banged on our door and told us—my parents, brother, and me—to get dressed and accompany them to the police station for identification purposes. My parents questioned the procedure but felt reasonably secure because of my father's position—business manager of Automotorul, the Ford franchise for all of Bukovina and northern Bessarabia—and because of my uncle's high-level connections. After we got dressed, my father grabbed his briefcase containing $250,000 cash of company money, and we left our home, never to see it again. It didn't even occur to my parents to offer the money as a bribe.

"In the courtyard, we were joined by some of our neighbors. We saw others holding bags of jewelry and negotiating with policemen. They stayed behind. We were trucked directly to the railroad station and sealed into a freight car. On the train my parents learned that the police had selected us at random in order to meet their quota of 200 people; they had fallen short because so many Jews had bought their way out.

"After travelling for about 24 hours without food, water, bedding, or sanitation, we discovered to our horror that the train had arrived at the Dniester River. After another day and night, we disembarked near an abandoned stone quarry deep in the Ukraine called Cariera de Piatra. We were assigned to barracks and put to work. The Romanian guards were vicious and used to beat people without provocation. My father entrusted the camp commander, a Romanian officer, with the cash-filled briefcase and informed him that my well-connected uncle was arranging our repatriation. The commander sent the briefcase with all its contents to Automotorul and confirmed to us that interventions had been made on our behalf.

"One grey autumn day we were ordered to bring all our belongings to the main camp area. The people felt no dread because they thought they were being relocated to other work camps. About 5,500 deportees lined up in the center square of the quarry, where five or six uniformed German officers sat behind tables, holding rosters. Trucks waited nearby. The camp commander approached my family and told us to get into one of the shacks near the barracks and to remain there. He told others the same thing, and they obeyed as we had. Soon the shacks were filled to capacity. After some time, it became very quiet outside. Suddenly we heard the voices of the Romanian commander, who was giving the Nazis some kind of explanation. The door opened and German faces peered inside. After more conversation, they left. Darkness fell and still we stood in silence, eerie silence.

"In the morning the camp guards called everyone to the square. We looked around and counted about 400–450 people. The commander arrived and, with tears in his eyes, announced, "I saved as many of you as I could. You have survived, and hopefully you will survive. The winter will be difficult, but we will do all we can. The worst is over."

"In the spring, the remaining deportees were moved from Cariera de Piatra to nearby villages and farms, where we remained until the liberation."

*Part Three*

---

# SPRING–SUMMER, 1942

REUNION
*Jagendorf Archives, Yad Vashem, The Holocaust Martyrs' and Heroes'
Remembrance Authority, Jerusalem*

# 1

---

# GARDEN OR
# GRAVEYARD?

THE PREFECT was neither friend nor adversary. If he had received an order to execute me, he would have complied, perhaps with regret. I tried my best not to compromise him. We danced on a tightrope: one slip by either, and both would fall. He had the upper hand in our macabre game. When he received an order affecting us, I had to decide, sometimes in an instant, whether to accept, bargain, or resist, always providing a rationale he could use to placate his superiors.

In March, 1942, Prefect Baleanu proposed a long-term solution to the problem of housing the Jews infiltrating Moghilev from the camps: the creation of an agricultural camp at Scazinet, several miles from the city. He estimated that 4,000 Jews could be billeted in the former military barracks. Excited by the prospect of a Jewish farm, I acquired authorizations to send to Scazinet a team of agricultural and technical advisers.

Scazinet turned out to be nothing more than two rows of dilapidated barracks surrounded by a large expanse of neglected land. Our advance team found not a single tractor or plough horse, not a trace of agricultural activity. They did find evidence of mass killings at the site. Despite its shortcomings, a possible food source for more than 15,000 starving people could not be dismissed lightly. Even if the authorities confiscated the harvest, we still could glean a portion for ourselves.

With the planting season drawing near, we quickly compiled a list of necessary farming tools, provisions, seeds, and construction materials. In a detailed report to Colonel Baleanu, we estimated the maximum capacity of the rebuilt barracks to be 2,500, allowing two square yards per person. We calculated that 1,500 settlers would work as farmhands on 200 acres, cultivating legumes, potatoes, corn, beans, and beet sugar. The remaining thousand would serve as support staff. Colonel Baleanu said he would need time to study our proposal.

Meanwhile, the winter death toll mounted. Piles of corpses stacked like cordwood awaited burial in the frozen earth. Our hope of survival was sustained by the Turnatoria, and now by the prospect of a farm.

We should have known that a benign prefect could not last long in Transnistria. We learned Colonel Baleanu would be dismissed. The secret service knew from the start about his business dealings with Jewish profiteers. Even more incriminating, he was considered too soft on Jews. Perhaps it was in reaction to this perception that his last act in office was one of betrayal. Knowing that his departure was imminent, he wired Governor Alexianu to propose the establishment of a new Lager in Scazinet for 4,000 Jews. The governor approved the plan promptly and issued an evacuation order effective April 22, 1942. I feared our spring garden would become a graveyard.

# 2

# A NEW PREFECT

T HE NEW prefect was the hardened anti-Semite Colonel Constantin Nasturas, a poet using the pen name Poiana-Volbure. He was a short man with a severe demeanor. At his first public act, Colonel Nasturas inspected the Turnatoria, after which he announced that I could continue as director.

Mr. Fuciu told me later that he and several local officials had told Colonel Nasturas about my initiatives in Moghilev and the Jewish contribution to the city's reconstruction. The authorities, he pointed out, would complain bitterly if they lost all the free labor.

"Believe me," said Mr. Fuciu, "the new prefect will learn quickly what your people can do for him. You have made the authorities in Moghilev feel that all your labors are for their benefit."

I pointed out that Colonel Nasturas will also learn quickly that Colonel Baleanu's demise resulted from his collaboration with Jews.

"Yes, but who would dare accuse Poiana-Volbure of pro-Jewish sympathies," replied Mr. Fuciu, "he's above reproach."

The new prefect arrived at the time of our greatest suffering. Statistics from November, 1941 through April 20, 1942 showed

3,410 dead, among them 267 children. Our hospital population had climbed to 3,777. The authorized Jewish population totaled 12,276, with the likely prospect that about one in three soon would be evacuated to Scazinet. Major Romeo Orasanu, the new commander of the legion of gendarmes, confirmed my worst fears regarding Scazinet: an edict of the governor was absolute. He counseled against my asking the prefect to seek cancellation of the decision, suggesting that I push instead for a postponement.

I sent Colonel Nasturas a copy of our field report, which described the deplorable living conditions in Scazinet and detailed the extensive renovations required to make the barracks habitable and the fields productive. Colonel Nasturas sought a postponement, but Governor Alexianu granted a reprieve of only a few days.

I handed the prefect a stronger appeal: "If Scazinet is to become an agricultural colony, even in a modest way, the barracks must be completely rebuilt . . . Also, there is no possibility of procuring food.

"Knowing your great spirit of humanity, Mr. Prefect, and referring to your hopeful words that it is not your intention to add to their misery, I trust you will reconsider the evacuation order.

"Most important, a delay is necessary due to the typhus epidemic. It will take weeks to disinfect everyone and quarantine those showing symptoms.

"I beg you to consider these factors, Mr. Prefect, and call for the revocation of the evacuation decree. If that is not possible, I request a delay of sufficient duration to allow for all necessary preparations."

Colonel Nasturas said he could do no more than extend the deadline a few more days. Then he told me to prepare a list of evacuees. I refused, saying neither I nor my staff would decide which Jews were to be sent to their deaths. I insisted that the authorities compile their own list and left the prefectura in despair.

It happened that the prefect's wife and daughter visited Turnatoria later that day. After giving them a personal tour, I asked Mrs. Nasturas to use her influence in helping us prevent a disaster. She promised to intercede. A few hours later the colonel informed me that he would seek another postponement.

We sought the intervention of the Jewish Center in Bucharest and enlisted the cooperation of Major Dr. C. Chirila, who, as a health ministry official, could demand that the deportation be delayed until disinfection procedures had been completed; otherwise, thousands of people, including soldiers, risked exposure to typhus. The doctor promised to intercede when the new evacuation date was announced.

Having done what I could to oppose the Scazinet decree, I returned to my routine in the Turnatoria, where the number of employees had dropped from 187 to 120 due to the epidemic. Notwithstanding the shortage of food, the frigid weather, and the typhus, we made enough progress in the first six months to ready the factory for operation. The buildings had been restored, tools made, offices furnished and painted, forms printed. We constructed a machine which used scrap from our sheet metal department to produce nails of all sizes, and soon supplied the entire district.

To keep additional workers busy, the Turnatoria organized a variety of trade shops. Jewish artisans engraved heirlooms, artists painted canvases. Our craftsmen and mechanics repaired watches, radios, cameras, even cars, but only as favors to officials who were inclined to reciprocate.

By the end of April, 1942, our committee had established public kitchens, an old-age home, three hospitals, two orphanages, a dental lab, a sanitation service, a pharmacy, and three bakeries. We received funds from Bucharest to establish similar services in the district Lager of Sargorod, Tropova, Murafa, Lucinet, Djurin, and Copaigorod. Our administration took the form of an autonomous state, with departments of finance, taxes, police, justice, records, census, post, sanitation, food procurement, labor, and burial.

In the period from December, 1941, through April, 1942, the committee's labor department provided the authorities with 35,993 man-hours. According to Ordinance No. 23, the work-

Cenzura Cernăuți No. 9

Dlui

Ing. S. Jaegendorf

Turnătoria

Moghilev

Transnistria

25. IV. 1942.

Sehr geehrter Herr Ing.!

*Postcard from Dr. Albert Pilpel in Cernauti to Jagendorf, dated April 4, 1942, thanking the Turnatoria director for locating his wife and daughter in a Transnistria concentration camp. Dr. Pilpel writes: "May God reward you for it."*

ers were entitled to receive food coupons valued at one or two RKKS marks per workday. We fought in vain to obtain these bonds, receiving only a fraction, and this only because of my excellent relationship with Moghilev's new mayor, Captain Nicolae Botta. In most camps the authorities enacted only the ordinance's punitive clauses, never the benefits.

# 3

## SPARING THE SCOUNDRELS

THE MOST feared man in Transnistria, Mihail P. Iliescu, chief of the inspectorate of gendarmes, came to Moghilev and demanded to know why the committee had not obeyed the governor's order to evacuate 4,000 Jews to Scazinet. I explained that the site was unfit for human habitation. Taken aback by my impudence, Colonel Iliescu wanted to know the duties of each committee member. He designated two of them as hostages and ordered that the evacuations proceed at once.

A three-man commission made up of Moghilev's inspector general of administration, Dimitrie Stefanescu; Prefect Nasturas; and the gendarme commander, Romeo Orasanu compiled the evacuation lists, supposedly beginning with persons known to have had commercial links with the former prefect or otherwise engaged in black market activities. Also high on the list were people from Cernauti, whom the Romanians automatically labeled Communists.

I implored Mr. Stefanescu to inspect Scazinet firsthand. He agreed and took along the prefect and gendarme commander. Upon their return, I asked Dimitrie Stefanescu if he still thought that human beings could survive in such a place. "If you had done what they had," he snapped, "you would be going there, too!"

I received written instructions on May 25, 1942, indicating the Stefanescu Commission's official evacuation priorities. The first to go would be "those who have committed unworthy acts during their stay in Moghilev"; second, "those who are rich and have the means of self support"; third, "Jews deported from Cernauti." Specialized factory workers, widows with children, and the destitute elderly would be exempted.

The instructions stipulated that the evacuees take along all their possessions. For each of the three transports the gendarme commander would provide thirty horse-drawn wagons for baggage and charge each evacuee a fee of two RKKS marks. The first convoy of 1,000 Jews would leave Moghilev on May 29, 1942, the second on May 31, and the last four days later. The convoys would be escorted by soldiers of the 13th Battalion, who would remain at the camp as guards and secure the perimeter with barbed wire supplied by the Jewish Committee. The transport would include ten doctors, ten rabbis, and five dentists. Jews were to have absolutely no contact with Romanian military or civil personnel or with the Ukrainians in the vicinity. Any Jew caught leaving the Lager would be shot as a spy. Failure to comply with these orders, I was warned, "could cost your head."

When the Stefanescu Commission posted its evacuation list, we noted that the scoundrels had been spared, while innocent people, including hospital patients, had been selected. My persistent protests to the prefect eventually reduced the number of evacuees from four thousand to three thousand.

The Scazinet upheaval provided Major Romeo Orasanu and his Jewish accomplices with an opportunity to sell exemptions to Jews who could afford to buy their way off the evacuation rolls. I considered filing a complaint against the gendarme commander, but how could we be sure that his successor would be any better, or that the scandal wouldn't backfire and engulf the entire colony? I applied what little leverage I could on the major. Whenever he denied a legitimate request, I asked him, "How come this or that one slated for Scazinet is still in Moghilev?" He would then grant my request, insisting on the innocence of the Jew in question.

Following the evacuations, Colonel Nasturas summoned me

to his office and requested my resignation as committee president. I refused, suspecting his motive was to quell my interventions concerning Scazinet.

"Don't be a fool Jagendorf, I want to save your life," he said, handing me a secret memorandum that had been sent to all prefects from the commander of the Third Romanian Army:

"We have the honor to inform you that the following orders must be observed as a means of preventing Jews from leaving their places of confinement. . . . If anyone escapes, the Jew in charge will be summarily executed. Each Lager chief must sign this order. You will take from each Lager in your district one Jew who has left his domicile without authorization and have him shot."

"Do you understand now?" the prefect asked. "I don't want you in a situation where neither I nor anyone else could save you. I will continue to support your efforts, even if you are not the official leader. I will need your decision today."

I requested time to consult with my advisers. Dr. Chirila counseled me to resign at once. In the Turnatoria, I met with Dr. Jonas Kessler, Dr. Hillel Brender, Max Heissman, David Rennert, and Pinkas Katz, who all advised me to step down. "But would you have me save my life by allowing another, perhaps one of you, to die?" I protested.

"It is not a question of honor but of saving Jewish lives," insisted one of them. "By resigning you still would be in a position to intervene in a crisis. No one but you could do that." I decided to resign on condition that my successor be forewarned of the personal risk. I proposed Dr. Josef Schauer, an attorney and former lumber baron who had a reputation for competency and decency.

The next day, I informed the prefect of my decision and requested an authorization for Dr. Schauer's transfer from Sargorod. When he arrived, I briefed him about the army memorandum and the job requirements. He accepted the position without hesitation, requesting only that I lend my active support. I resigned on June 16, 1942.

No more than 3,000 Jews actually went to Scazinet. Once the matter was out of Stefanescu's hands, we arranged aid for the

Scazinet people and brought back the sick to Moghilev. The excitement over Scazinet subsided and the Lager was dissolved in September, 1942, thankfully before the onset of winter. Some of the people were dispatched to other camps in the district but most returned to Moghilev.

# 4

---

# CHEATING THE
# EXECUTIONER

In early June, 1942, a seventeen-year-old kitchen worker named Rifka Laster asked to see me about a matter of great urgency. Her friend, Arnold Auerbach, had been caught attempting to enter Moghilev illegally and was to be executed that night at 10 P.M. I rushed to the gendarmerie and appealed to Major Orasanu for Mr. Auerbach's release.

"How can I release him when the law demands his head?" asked the commander.

"Because as a human being you would not kill a son for attempting to see his dying mother. He could not get an authorization; what was he to do? What would you have done in his place?"

After a long discussion, Major Orasanu agreed to free Auerbach, but he took offense at my insistence that the prisoner leave with me.

"Do you doubt my word?" complained the major.

"Not at all," I said. "I merely want to take him to see his mother."

"Very well," he said, ordering the jailer to release Auerbach. In truth, I accompanied him because gendarmes often did their dirty work at night and apologized for "the error" in the morning. I took Arnold Auerbach into the Turnatoria as a foundry worker. After the war, he married Rifka and eventually they made their home in Paris.

More complicated was the case of the Costiners—a family divided between Moghilev and Tulcin. I was particularly eager to arrange for their reunification because one of the Costiners in Tulcin had technical skills we needed. After obtaining approval for the transfer, I rented a truck and hired a police sergeant to escort the Costiners to Moghilev. He returned alone and handed me a note from the Tulcin gendarme commander: "We have the honor to report that the Jew, Abraham Jacques Costiner and four members of his family—Henry, Ruth, Sali, and Elmano—were handed over to the Germans as laborers on August 18, 1942, by order of the prefect of Tulcin. They crossed the Bug River along with approximately 3,000 Jews."

We knew that the Germans routinely shot Jewish workers upon completion of their assignments. Though my chances of retrieving the Costiners were slim, I rushed to Mr. Fuciu's office and asked him to arrange a letter from the German commander in Moghilev to his counterpart in the camp across the Bug, requesting the immediate transfer of the five Costiners. Mr. Fuciu obtained the order, which I gave to the sergeant. That night, the truck carrying the Costiners arrived in Moghilev, and not a moment too soon. The shootings had already begun. Of the 3,000 Jews sent over the Bug from Tulcin, only the five Costiners survived.

# 5

---

# TRAINING
# THE YOUTH

During my eight-month tenure, we had restored the city's electricity and brought the Turnatoria to a state of production readiness. The factory now employed 300 workers and sheltered 2,500 dependents. With the bitter winter behind them, our people began to regain confidence.

The factory apprenticeship program gave our youth an opportunity to learn a trade. An admissions committee selected candidates, judging them according to physical, mental, moral, and economic criteria. The committee submitted its recommendations to me for approval. When faced with a choice, I took the applicant who needed the job to survive over the one with superior qualifications. The "cadets" divided their day between work and study in our technical school. Professional teachers taught them theoretical subjects, and engineers provided instruction in applied sciences. It gave me great satisfaction to see young people learning trades that would enable them to find jobs after the liberation and support their families.

Most Jews in Moghilev knew nothing about the course of the war, which ultimately would settle our fate. Optimism healed, but it also infected many with a careless arrogance.

The racketeers who evaded Scazinet saw no reason to change their ways. A class of women appeared in the street arrayed in fancy clothes; they passed the time playing cards. Such shameless behavior could only be viewed by the regime as an affront.

One of our chemists had set up a still in the factory basement to produce alcohol for disinfection purposes during the epidemic. After the government began providing us with the precious commodity, we bartered our homemade liquor for food, retaining some to celebrate weddings, engagements, marriages, and birthdays—the rare occasions when we suspended our sorrows.

On August 1, 1942, my 57th birthday, I found on my desk the following letter, signed, "The 4-cylinder motor with 50 H.P."

"Mr. Engineer:

The undersigned has the honor to report that for almost a year I have nothing to eat but the dregs of Russian oil. To make matters worse, my weary body has absorbed many a blow. Considering the above, I respectfully request (1) formation of a committee of doctors and nurses to study my health history and put me on the payroll, (2) enroll me as an apprentice to learn how to diagnose my defects, and (3) place me on the list of ailing workers who need a nutritional supplement every morning at ten."

One motor, in particular, had given us much trouble. After replacing its missing parts, we still could not get it started. Weeks later, we discovered that the Russians had poured sand into the fuel line. As soon as the line was unclogged, the motor functioned perfectly. The episode now could be recalled with a smile.

We had made great progress in our relations with the initially hostile Ukrainian population. When they ran afoul of the Romanian and German authorities, they often sought and received our help. We employed them in the Turnatoria, apprenticed their children, and allowed them access to our social service organizations. In appreciation, they sold us milk and food, often on credit.

Even the Germans treated us better. In the beginning they tormented anyone who passed by wearing the obligatory Star of David. They delighted in sadistic games. A Jew who failed to salute a German risked a severe beating or worse, but so did a Jew who dared to insult a German with a "Jew-greeting." Germans who abused our people received little cooperation from me when they came to the foundry requesting personal favors—a radio repaired, a silver watch engraved, toys for their children, and the like.

The Romanian leadership in Transnistria made a career of tormenting us. One day the prefect informed me that the governor wanted all rabbis in Moghilev liquidated because supposedly they had been praying for a Soviet victory. After enlisting Major Orasanu's cooperation, I ordered the immediate closing of all synagogues. The next day a delegation of outraged rabbis stormed into my office demanding an explanation. I could not reveal my reason, but told them that the action was in their best interest. Closing the synagogues satisfied the governor, and spared the rabbis, who never learned the motive for my action.

The war-stricken economy was in a shambles. The local population could not make even the most simple repairs. By the end of summer, 1942, the Turnatoria was in full operation and vital to the regional economy. We manufactured and stockpiled farm tools and a variety of scarce replacement parts. As the demand for our products increased, we expanded all departments and our capacity to fabricate customized fittings. Factory orders arrived from all over Transnistria. We manufactured equipment for sugar factories and thousands of piston rings for tractors. To meet the growing demand, we added a second shift and employed our cadets. With the factory expansion came a significant improvement in our quality of life. The collective farms, which depended on our services, paid in produce for machine parts. Each Turnatoria member now could purchase provisions on credit from our food store.

When the Germans or Romanians requested we manufacture armaments, we contrived various excuses: lack of raw material, defective machinery, inexperience. The Turnatoria produced not a single item that could be used in battle. In repairing farm equipment, however, we did contribute indirectly to the Nazi war effort. On the positive side, our actions fed the occupied Ukrainian population and, most importantly, kept us alive.

# 6

## THE CRUCIFIX

ONE MORNING Colonel Nasturas came to the factory and proposed that we construct a grand monument to memorialize the
Romanian soldiers who fell in the vicinity of Moghilev. It would
stand on the highway to Sargorod with a view of the Dniester. I
saw the request as an opportunity to gain public recognition for
our artistic and engineering proficiency. A sketch by Architect
Kurzweil proposing a wood-sculpted crucifix pleased the prefect. I used the occasion to wrest some concessions from Colonel
Nasturas, but, whenever I asked for rations to feed the 1,500
children in our three orphanages, he contrived some excuse. His
callousness so infuriated me that once I blurted out, "Mr. Prefect, did you ever think of the possibility that history will record
that the famous Romanian writer Poiana-Volbure caused the
deaths of hundreds of orphaned children only because they
were born Jews?" My outburst unsettled the prefect. He asked
me how the war was going.

"I don't know. Remember, we are forbidden to read newspapers or listen to radios."

"Come now, you know full well what's going on in the world,
and I would appreciate your telling me . . . confidentially of
course."

"In that case, I will tell you that America's entry into the war will shift the balance. Hitler's days are numbered."

"What do you think will happen to Romania?"

"Don't worry, Marshal Antonescu will say that Hitler forced him into the alliance."

Sobered by our exchange, the prefect asked, "What is it you needed for the orphanages?" I handed him the requisition, and he signed it.

Early the next morning, Mayor Nicolae Botta came to my office and, shutting the door, said, "I thought you were a shrewd man, but what you did yesterday proved me wrong."

"What happened?"

"A terrible thing, and I am afraid it will have grave consequences for you. Yesterday, while dining at the club, the prefect told us, in the presence of Germans, that you were predicting Hitler would lose the war. They will have your head for that. I suggest you flee while you can."

After explaining how my remark came about, I rejected the mayor's advice and told him we would have to wait and see. Nothing happened. The prefect had not intended to hurt me; he simply had failed to grasp the implications of his words.

Intimidation was an inescapable reality in Moghilev. We did not know when the next blow would strike, only that it would. One morning a squad of Romanian soldiers entered the Turnatoria compound and cordoned off the perimeter. Colonel Mihail P. Iliescu, the feared chief of the inspectorate of gendarmes, flanked by high-ranking officers, marched into my office. He demanded an accounting of all workers present. I handed him the daily report, which he examined without comment. He thumbed through several ledgers and stacks of blueprints, then asked to see each department and shop. At every station, he observed diligent workers. When we entered the shop where a Jewish artisan was meticulously carving the cross, the colonel's demeanor softened.

We continued through the factory living quarters, the pharmacy and medical division, the kitchen and storehouses, the schools and orphanages. At the prefectura Colonel Iliescu con-

fided that he had never seen Jews engaged in productive labor.
I told him that our only desire was to be allowed to work without interference. He told me that another round of evacuations
was being planned but offered no details. I did not press him,
satisfied to have mollified so powerful an adversary.

---

# Spring–Summer, 1942

IN THE spring of 1942, Hitler ordered his generals to plan a summer offensive in Russia, targeting Stalingrad, a vital industrial center on the Volga. The British launched a massive aerial attack on Germany at the end of May, after signing a treaty with the U.S.S.R. The United States declared war on Romania on June 5, 1942.

In their campaign against the Jews, fascist forces advanced virtually unopposed. March, 1942, marked the beginning of mass deportations of Jews to the gas chambers at Auschwitz-Birkenau. Moreover, the mass shootings continued in occupied Soviet territory.

By May, 1942, the Romanian government had forced the Jewish minority to "contribute" to state coffers an estimated two billion lei ($10,000,000), in addition to massive quantities of bedding and clothing. Jews who could not meet their assessments were jailed. In January, 1943, the Jewish community ransomed the prisoners for one hundred million lei ($500,000). In addition, individual Jews paid government officials a fortune to avoid forced labor.

In August, 1942, Marshal Antonescu and his deputy, Mihai Antonescu, secretly consented to Germany's request that the Jews of the Old Kingdom and southern Transylvania be deported to Poland, where they would be liquidated. The German embassy in Bucharest announced the details of the agreement in its official newspaper, the *Bukarester Tageblatt*, dismaying the Romanian leadership. Germany's persistent demands for more oil, more grain, and more soldiers (approximately a half million would die), while totally disregarding Romania's political objectives, particularly the recovery of northern Transylvania from Hungary, alienated Bucharest from Berlin. Romanian resentment was deepened after Berlin had bungled a visit by Radu Lecca, the Romanian commissar for Jewish questions. Foreign ministry officials in the German capital snubbed the Romanian envoy, believing that the matter of deporting the balance of Romanian Jewry to Belzec was a fait accompli.

Exploiting the government's ebbing enthusiasm for the Nazi-initiated deportation of Romanian Jews to gas chambers in Poland, Dr. Filderman framed the Jewish question in terms of national honor. He argued that Germany had no right to demand that Romania, an ally, surrender her entire Jewish population. The same demand had not been made at that time of Hungary. Jewish leaders also floated the idea that world Jewry would pay a king's ransom to redeem Romania's Jews for resettlement in Palestine. It was this intermingling of factors combined with external pressures from the Swiss, Vatican, Americans and others, that induced Bucharest to begin formulating a more independent policy in dealing with its Jewish minority. As a result, approximately 350,000 of Romania's 760,000 Jews survived the Holocaust.

---

Moghilev's bone-chilling winter was followed by a stormy spring with torrential rains and high winds. The typhus pandemic persisted, causing alarm that it might spread to military personnel. Colonel Baleanu ordered an inspection of Jewish-operated facilities in March, 1942, and called upon the committee to take strict regulatory measures. He insisted that the Jewish leadership be more forceful in keeping people off the streets and putting them to work. He ordered that unsanitary Jewish food stalls be closed, criticized the filthy conditions in the hospitals, demanded payment for illegal electrical hook-ups, and questioned the presence of eighty Jewish workers in the Turnatoria when a third of that number would have sufficed. The committee launched its own investigation and found widespread abuses.

In a confidential memo dated May 6, 1942, Jagendorf accused a Jewish hospital director of inadequate supervision. The facility fell under scrutiny following the death of a patient who had been administered the wrong drug by an unauthorized nurse. Jagendorf initiated an inquiry and insisted the supervising physician be fired. "There are many doctors in the hospital," Jagendorf wrote, "and it is they who should be administering the injections. . . . You have to introduce a system whereby every doctor must be present from at least 7:30 A.M. to 2:00 P.M. . . . We must dismiss those doctors who neglect their duties in fighting the epidemic. . . . You also must be more vigilant in guarding provisions. We are doing everything in our power to feed the sick, but the food is stolen by the medical staff. . . . The hospital was established for the sake of the sick, not for disreputable doctors who exploit it to recruit private patients. . . ."

On April 4, 1942, the Jewish Committee in Moghilev opened the first orphanage in Transnistria. Dr. Shmuel Ben-Zion, author of a doctoral dissertation on the Jewish orphans of Transnistria, found that Jagendorf had dedicated himself fully to protecting the unprotected children, channeling half the committee's financial resources into the orphanages. Ben-Zion told me the following story to illustrate his point:

"A group from the Jewish Committee appropriated a ton of firewood from the orphan home for private use. As the rumor spread through Moghilev that the children had no fuel, Jagendorf ordered an immediate investigation and demanded the culprits replace the stack within 24 hours. The wood materialized miraculously, well ahead of the deadline."

---

The Scazinet (Skah-zee-nets) affair cost Jagendorf a loss of prestige among his own people and prompted his resignation from the Jewish Committee on June 16, 1942. Apparently, Jagendorf had been duped by Colonel Baleanu, whom he had regarded as relatively benevolent. Seeking to convince Governor Gheorghe Alexianu that he was no Jew-lover, the embattled Baleanu conceived of a radical plan to liquidate almost one-third of Moghilev's Jews. The prefect probably had no intention of establishing a farm; Scazinet was to be a death trap.

The new prefect of Moghilev, Colonel Constantin Nasturas (Nahs-tuh-rash), presided over the Scazinet evacuations, ordering the first group of 1,000 evacuees to gather with their belongings on May 29, 1942, near the Jewish cemetery on the Moghilev–Sargorod road. A second convoy left two days later. As the evacuees trudged through knee-deep mud, gendarmes whipped and beat them. At "the Sargorod Hill," the victims struggled on their hands and knees to mount the sliding slope. The remaining 2,500 deportees left Moghilev for Scazinet on June 4, 1942. An additional five hundred Jews were drawn from other district camps to complete the 4,000 quota.

Enclosed by barbed wire, Scazinet was guarded by Ukrainian militia, Romanian gendarmes, and Jewish police; nonetheless, a small number of Jews managed to flee. Survivor Jacob Vogel told me in a telephone interview from Cleveland, Ohio what happened after he and a friend escaped the camp:

"We were hiding in a tall cornfield when suddenly we heard, 'Halt, hands up.' Two young Romanian soldiers were pointing their rifles at us. One of them shouted, "You are Communist spies." We pleaded for our lives, explaining that we left Scazinet only to find food. The soldiers searched us and found the prayerbook I had received for my bar mitzvah. One of them pointed to it and said, 'You see, he's got Communist literature.' The other soldier recognized the script as Hebrew and said, 'If he keeps a prayerbook in his pocket, then he's not a Communist. Let them go. I don't want to have their deaths on my conscience.' "

The living quarters in Scazinet consisted of two rows of barracks. On one side of the road the barracks had been reconstructed; on the other side they were without roofs, windows, and doors. Twice a week, barrels of soup made from animal feed were delivered from Moghilev in carts drawn by Jewish men. Even at Scazinet, some of the evacuees found ways to procure money from relatives. They opened stands, selling cornbread and other provisions purchased from Ukrainian peasants who had entered the camp illegally. The majority of the inmates fed on grass and bark. Soon not a trace of green remained. In digging for water, the inmates unearthed decaying corpses. (The previous summer, German troops had murdered approximately 9,000 deported Bessarabian Jews at the site.)

An estimated 2,500 of the Moghilev deportees perished in Scazinet before Governor Gheorghe Alexianu closed the camp on September 12, 1942. Of the approximately 1,500 survivors, only a handful of specialists returned to Moghilev; the majority were dispersed to three concentration camps near the Bug River; their fate is unknown. Those too sick to travel were left to die at the camp.

In his memoir, Jagendorf downplayed the Scazinet catastrophe, indicating that most of the evacuees had survived their ordeal. To his credit, however, Jagendorf had strongly resisted the evacuation order, refusing to prepare the lists demanded by Moghilev's inspector general of administration, Dimitrie Stefanescu. He also spoke forcefully to the dreaded Colonel Iliescu. When it became clear to Jagendorf that he had lost his battle to stay the evacuations, he admonished Colonel Nasturas with these words:

"If it were a matter of transporting cattle, you would take care to properly prepare them so as not to endanger their lives. I ask you, Mr. Prefect, why can't you extend the same fundamental right to these poor people?"

Jagendorf reproached the hardhearted prefect on a second matter as well: his cruel disregard for the plight of the orphans. Shmuel Ben-Zion believes that a major reason for Jagendorf's resignation was "his inability to resolve the orphan problem."

---

Outwardly, Jagendorf demonstrated loyalty to the Romanian cause, thereby gaining the respect and confidence of even the most ardent anti-Semites in Transnistria. Aside from the Turnatoria itself, nothing pleased the militarists more than Architect Samuel Kurzweil's monumental crucifix, which paid tribute to Marshal Antonescu and memorialized the fallen Romanian and German soldiers in the war against the Soviets. To the Jews, the cross erected just east of the city symbolized their own Calvary, victims of Rome resurrected.

Constructed of solid oak, the cross's horizontal beam supported an iron replica of Marshal Antonescu's sword. The forty-foot vertical column displayed helmets representing the heroic Romanian and German soldier. At the base lay a memorial book cast in bronze, its open pages inscribed with the words: "And it is written in the eternal book that countries and people perish, but our dear Romania eternally will flourish." Jewish workers drew an electric line to illuminate the monument for its dedication on November 3, 1942. The event received notice in the Romanian press, but no mention was made of Jewish involvement; all credit went to Colonel Constantin Nasturas.

---

Jagendorf's memoir ignores the religious dimension of the exile. Thousands of devout Jews turned to God for deliverance. In Moghilev, deportees rebuilt demolished synagogues and attended worship services whenever possible. Dr. Avigdor Shachan wrote in *Burning Ice* that many of the exiled rabbis viewed the catastrophe mystically and, by their moral and spiritual example, served as "a source of encouragement to the multitudes with whom they marched through the fields of Transnistria, in the ghettos and work camps. . . . The believers were the first to overcome their shock . . . and organize themselves." They held to dietary laws, even if it meant starvation. They recited the Mourner's Kaddish in memory of the dead and gathered faithfully to observe the Day of Atonement, Yom Kippur. Although the Romanian authorities in Transnistria punished Jews who engaged in daily prayer and holiday observance, the pious clung to God and Torah.

---

Jagendorf makes no mention of a meeting held August 20–21, 1942, attended by thirty-five Jewish representatives from two dozens camps. The delegates, many of whom arrived by foot, met to discuss the creation of a district-wide assistance committee. According to Shraga (Jurgrau) Yeshurun, author of a study on the self-administration of the Moghilev ghetto:

"Siegfried Jagendorf (who at the time held no official position on the Moghilev Jewish Committee) opened the meeting with a speech stressing that the basis for Jewish existence in Transnistria was productive labor, which demonstrated to the authorities the usefulness of Jews. He also emphasized that social help had to be provided to those who were unfit for work: orphans, women with young children, and the old people. Those capable of work had to be fed in public canteens, and sanitary services were required to quarantine those with infectious diseases. The keynote speaker ended by warning delegates that he would not hesitate to inform the authorities about any colony chief who abused the public trust. . . .

"Dr. Josef Schauer (Jagendorf's successor) followed with a survey of his committee's activities in the city of Moghilev. The other delegates then reported on conditions in their colonies and agreed to conduct a census in anticipation of receiving material relief from the Jewish Center. They complained about the inequitable system of distributing financial aid from Jewish sources in Romania to the camps and warned that they would hold the Jewish Center responsible if the second winter turned out to be as catastrophic as the first. . . .

"A circular letter and a questionnaire had been distributed to the delegates (at the initiative of the Jewish Center and Jagendorf) stating that assistance would be given as a condition of their instituting communal kitchens, pharmacies, hospitals, and other communal services. Jagendorf announced the appointment of Isidor Pressner, Josef Schauer, and Alfred Kapise to serve with him on the newly formed District Committee of Assistance. During the gathering of colony representatives, no one objected to these appointments. However, Meyer Teich, who boycotted the meeting, wrote a letter from Sargorod objecting to the selection process as a violation of the rules set forth in a letter from the Jewish Center, dated July 30, 1942. He criticized Jagendorf for failing to consult with the colony heads before naming the other three members, all of whom were concentrated in the same place—Moghilev. Moreover, Teich accused the Moghilev committee of confiscating and delaying distribution of assistance funds and medicines earmarked for the district Lager. The Sargorod leader concluded by protesting Jagendorf's allegations that colony chiefs had betrayed the public trust. Teich refused to recognize the new assistance committee until these sweeping accusations of corruption were properly investigated. The dispute remained unresolved, and the assistance committee collapsed."

Jagendorf's resignation from the Jewish Committee did not constitute a surrender of power; he merely shed a title that invited Jewish recrimination and Romanian retribution. During Dr. Shauer's tenure as president, Jagendorf continued to maintain close contacts with the Romanian authorities in Moghilev and with the Jewish Center in Bucharest. All the while, he held the prestigious directorship of the Turnatoria, his real power base.

On August 29, 1942, Jagendorf wrote to a friend in Switzerland, "My activity gives me much joy because it is supported and recognized by important authorities. I now hold the position that I held before the war . . . though not from the standpoint of my previous financial success. We have everything and do not need anything."

*Part Four*

---

# FALL, 1942

**Soup Kitchen**

*Jagendorf Archives, Yad Vashem, The Holocaust Martyrs' and Heroes'
Remembrance Authority, Jerusalem*

# 1

# A GRAND
# SCHEME

THE THIRTY Ukrainians who worked in the Turnatoria received, on paper at least, five times the pay of Jews. Ordinance No. 23 kept us from gaining an equitable return for our contribution to the economy of Transnistria. Only the governor could amend the ordinance. I knew that Colonel Nasturas would not intervene, careful to avoid the stigma of being a Jew-lover. We needed an advocate in Odessa, the capital of Transnistria.

The opportunity came September 1, 1942, when the deputy governor for labor, Dr. Balkas, arrived in Moghilev to discuss plans for an exposition in Bucharest of goods produced in Transnistria. Dr. Balkas seemed like a decent man, one who might be open to my recommendations. First, I gave him a tour of the Turnatoria and the nail factory. Afterwards, he inspected the recently completed community trade shops—tailor, barber, shoemaker, knitter, watchmaker, cabinetmaker, chemist, and others. At the end of the tour, I broached the subject of the wage inequity. He promised to look into the matter. Then I introduced the idea of establishing a central Jewish labor office for all of Transnistria. He expressed interest and requested a formal proposal.

Mr. Balkas left Moghilev with the highest praise for our work. I felt confident that his report to Governor Alexianu and to the director of Industry would hasten the centralization of Jewish labor in all of Transnistria, and the Turnatoria would serve as the model. According to my scheme, the director of industry for Transnistria, Ion Fotiade, would have ultimate jurisdiction in all matters regarding Jewish work assignments. My objective was to remove the deportees from the caprice of corrupt local authorities.

I worked up the following proposal and sent it with a diagram to Mr. Balkas:

"A central office for the coordination of the Jewish work force in the whole of Transnistria must be created. This office will be under the jurisdiction of the labor director for Transnistria, who will determine work assignments in coordination both with the local authorities and Jewish committees. . . . At the earliest possible date, the central labor office will register all Jews in Transnistria and list their trade or profession. The office will work up a general plan for industrial workers, tradespeople, farm workers, and others who can be sent where they are needed regardless of their current domicile. For instance, the central labor office could send qualified personnel to the Turnatoria in Moghilev, which now runs three shifts and needs more specialists. . . .

"Specialists should be sent to existing industries in order to increase production and lower costs, to new enterprises, to remodel and rebuild destroyed factories, etc.

"New stores and shops should be created in cities lacking mechanics and tradespeople. The following enterprises are recommended: carriage building, cabinet making, auto repairing, locksmithing, rope making, book binding, and photography; also, construction teams would be formed to restore damaged buildings and erect new ones, as was done in Moghilev, where Jews repaired the prefectura, city hall, and many other office buildings. Upon completion of the reconstruction projects, these workers could be transferred to industrial jobs.

"Compensation must be settled at once. Only a fraction of the wages promised to Jews under Ordinance No. 23 has been paid to them. In Moghilev for work valued at 158,535 RKKS marks ($47,560), we have received only 21,483 RKKS marks ($6,445) in food bonds. In other districts, Jewish workers have realized nothing in return for their labors. To remedy this situation, the distribution of food bonds for each worker, at the minimum in accordance with Ordinance No. 23, must be organized within the framework of the central labor office and its district branches. The problem of nourishment is closely connected with productivity. . . . Therefore, the government must take the necessary steps to fulfill its obligation, so that workers do not go to their jobs with stomachs empty.

"In conclusion, I request cessation of all evacuations (from Moghilev); dissolution of all Lager, particularly Scazinet. (Article 2 of Ordinance No. 23 stipulates that the deported Jews be housed in empty, abandoned houses, not Lager, which are the seats of infections, hunger, and misery); enlargement of the ghetto in Moghilev; employment of Jewish specialists, male and female, in industries and shops, and untrained Jews in other jobs; the provision of heating fuel for the families of working Jews and institutions such as orphanages and hospitals; authorization to the Jewish Center in Bucharest to send clothes, bedding, and window glass to Moghilev; provision of all kinds of tools; and the means to maintain our social welfare institutions.

On September 23, 1942, Colonel Nasturas informed me that the governor of Transnistria and the German commander would be arriving the following day to inspect the Turnatoria. We rushed into action, changing our production schedule to showcase our most technically advanced products.

The next day, the prefect introduced me to the governor. To my surprise, Professor Gheorghe Alexianu shook my hand— the hand of a Jew wearing a Star of David. The German commander followed suit. I guided them and their entourage on a complete tour of the factory from raw material to shipping. In the foundry department, they observed how molten steel was cast into machine parts. In the adjoining building they watched lathes transform the castings into precision fittings. In the punchpress department, the governor saw metal fabricated into farm implements. In the carpenter shop, where a sculptor was completing the forty-foot crucifix, the governor lauded the achievement and shook my hand a second time. Perhaps, at that moment, the governor and German commander realized how wrong they had been about the Jews.

On October 5, 1942, the Bucharest newspaper *Currentul* featured a photograph of the cross and a brief article about the governor's tour of the Turnatoria, stating that the "inspected workers manufacturing a wide array of machine parts . . . and ordered this large industrial center to accelerate production. . . ." The report made no mention of the fact that deported Jews created this industrial wonder.

The governor's vote of confidence brought us comfort, the feeling that our chances for survival had improved. One incident confirmed this view. Captain Botez, my informant in the Romanian secret service, told me that the Third Romanian Army had ordered all Jews in Moghilev to be handed over to the Germans on October 5, 1942, but Governor Alexianu had rejected the proposal. After inspecting the Turnatoria, he must have concluded we served his purposes better alive than dead. Several weeks later, the governor and Marshal Ion Antonescu signed an order creating a central Jewish labor organizing office for the whole of Transnistria based on the formula I had presented to Dr. Balkas.

Romanian policy in Transnistria followed no consistent course; even as the Department of Industry endorsed the value of organized Jewish labor, the army or security police conspired to crush us. In early October, 1942, the secret service ordered Colonel Nasturas to evacuate 3,000 Jews from Moghilev to the death Lager in Peciora. News of the impending evacuation sent the Jewish population into a panic, driving many underground. Dr. Schauer pleaded with Major Orasanu to delay the evacuation, contending that the loss of so many Jews would throw the colony into disarray. Dr. Schauer won a reduction of 500 souls, but Moghilev's gendarme commander resisted further intercessions, accusing the Jews of parasitism and black marketeering. As in the past, the real Jewish parasites enjoyed the protection of their Romanian liaisons and had little to fear. Always the poorest of Jews, those unable to pay bribes, were the ones to be sacrificed. The destitute local Jews were a prime target because the Romanians regarded them all as Communists.

The roundups for Peciora began on October 12, 1942. Two weeks later, Dr. Schauer resigned as president, weary of battling Jewish racketeers who conspired to seize control of the Jewish committee. The community again turned to me. Having no desire to embroil myself in the factionalism, I refused. One delegation after another urged me to reconsider. The prefect added his voice, assuring me that the threat from the Third Army that had prompted my resignation no longer was a concern. I resumed the leadership in mid-December, 1942, in my new capacity as distict chief of the central office of Jewish labor, a position under the authority of the director of industry in Odessa. My committee consisted of Mihail Danilof, Dr. Jonas Kessler, Moses Katz, and Josef Laufer.

# 2

---

# PARTISANS AND
# TRAITORS

T HE RUSSIAN partisans who were concentrated in the forests
north of Moghilev aided Jews in the camps. Dr. Meyer Teich
kept in close contact with the resistance near Sargorod, as I did
in Moghilev. If Ukrainians mistreated Jews or refused to barter
or sell them food, the partisans sometimes intervened and punished the offenders. We provided the guerillas with soap, medicine, and other supplies. Many of the partisans worked in town
by day as truck drivers or mechanics and fought the Germans
after dark. A number of deportees joined the resistance movement as translators. The Axis forces had to divert a consider-
able number of units in attempting to eradicate the partisans,
but all such efforts failed.

Whenever partisans captured a German or Romanian unit,
they asked the soldiers if their commander had mistreated
them. If the men said yes, the partisans executed the officer
and released the soldiers after stripping them of their weapons
and uniforms.

One day the partisans captured a Romanian patrol near
Moghilev. The commander and one hundred soldiers returned
in their underwear. The Romanian intelligence officer investigating the incident asked the officer how he and his men com-

municated with the Russians. He said Romanian-speaking Jews had acted as translators. This revelation easily could have induced Antonescu to order our immediate liquidation. That night I sent a doctor to convince the investigating officer, a young and decent man, to strike the damning information from the record. Realizing how many lives were at stake, he complied, thus averting a catastrophe.

The same young officer helped us on another occasion as well. We needed access to news about world events, but newspapers and radios were strictly forbidden to Jews. Our underground communications with Bucharest were limited to matters of relief. Occasionally, our shop received a radio for repair, which we kept as long as possible for intelligence gathering, but we needed a continuous information source. I asked the young investigator to acquire a short-wave radio at our expense on his next trip to Bucharest or Cernauti. He insisted on buying the radio with his own funds and keeping it in his possession. We installed an electric line to his house and every night at 8:00 P.M. sent a doctor to monitor reports from New York, London, Moscow, and Berlin.

# 3

---

# THE CIGARETTE
# LIGHTER

On November 3, 1942, Mr. Fuciu came to the factory and ushered me into the large meeting hall, which doubled as our technical school. Inside, I was greeted by the department heads and a festive crowd. In commemoration of the first anniversary of our entering the Turnatoria, I was presented with a delicately engraved cigarette lighter and a letter of gratitude signed by hundreds of people. The letter memorialized the workers who died of starvation and disease in the first weeks, and pledged loyalty to my guiding principle: "Fewer words and more facts."

Mr. Fuciu also received a Turnatoria-made lighter, causing something of a scandal; soon every official, from the prefect down, clamored for a lighter. I refused hundreds of requests, explaining that the Turnatoria had to meet production deadlines. We made exceptions only for the top officials—those who held our fate in their hands.

Anticipating that the workers and even department heads would start manufacturing the lighters privately, I posted warnings that anyone caught dealing in them would be fired. I stepped up undercover surveillance of the Turnatoria and conducted more inspections myself. These actions sparked strong opposition from workers who accused me of denying them an opportunity to feed their families. I made many enemies. They did not realize that if the practice continued, we all would be accused of stealing government property—a capital offense.

Confirming my fears, a high-ranking military police officer appeared in my factory office one morning to inquire about the illegal manufacture of lighters. I told him that we had been investigating this problem ourselves for months and called in the man in charge. Handing the officer a thick file, our investigator explained that Ukrainians had stolen our design and were manufacturing lighters throughout the district. After a perfunctory examination of the file, the officer said, "I believe you are doing a good job. Send me your final report." At the door he turned and asked, "You don't happen to have an extra one of those lighters, do you?" "Just one," I told him, "which we confiscated yesterday." I reached into my drawer and handed it to him. He thanked me and left. I felt relieved but bitter about having to wage a war on two fronts—against our real enemies and against workers who thought only of themselves.

Moghilev was not for the naive. One afternoon, two strangers approached me on the street as I walked from the committee office to the Turnatoria. They introduced themselves as architects from Bucharest and said they had brought something for me. We arranged a rendezvous for later that afternoon but I forgot about it. The following day, I went so see the prefect and noticed the two architects seated in his waiting room. I apologized for my lapse. They assured me everything was fine, adding that they had encountered a friend of mine and had given him a bundle of letters intended for me. I did not tell them that they had been duped by a police informer. In the morning, I learned that the two architects had been arrested, along with three hundred Jews. I worked more than two weeks to win the release of our people. The ill-fated architects, however, received prison terms of twenty-five years at hard labor.

I wanted to have the informer eliminated. The opportunity came when he was arrested and charged for some unrelated offense. A military court in Cernauti sentenced him to a one year prison term. When he returned to Moghilev, I asked the police to transfer him to the Smerinca Lager. He was shot on arrival.

A second Jewish informer, younger and even more dangerous, terrorized our people. I tried unsuccessfully to reform him. He insisted on becoming police chief. When I refused, he tried to intimidate me, so I requested his transfer to a Lager, citing infractions of ordinances and refusal to work. The military police knew why I wanted him out of the way. Since his intelligence value had been compromised, the police disposed of him in the Dniester River. Thus did we rid ourselves of two traitors who compounded our suffering. Every people has its criminals; we Jews are no exception.

After the war, the executioners of the second informer were charged in the killing. The prosecutor asked me for information about the incident. I testified that the victim was a traitor who deserved to die and called for the defendants' release. My recommendation was accepted and the case closed.

# 4

---

# THE STOLEN BELT

ONE MORNING upon arriving at the Turnatoria, I received devastating news. Thieves had made off with the twenty-inch-wide leather belt that drove the machines in the lathe and power plant department. As a result, 150 workers stood idle and the plant ceased production. No piece cast in the foundry or worked up in the other departments could be finished. The missing belt was the factory's main artery, linking the diesel electromotor, our only power source, to a long transmission belt that ran the lathe, drills, and other machines.

It was obviously an inside job because we had round-the-clock guards watching the installation. I didn't want the Romanian authorities to find out. They would have regarded the incident as an act of sabotage. I asked the plant superintendent, Mr. Pinkas Katz to rig up a makeshift belt and run the department at reduced capacity. Then I ordered our factory detective and intelligence men to recover the belt before the shoemakers got hold of it. In less than an hour, we knew who stole the belt and to whom it was sold. But it already had been cut to pieces.

We could not conceal the crime, since hundreds of workers, including more than thirty Ukrainians, knew what had happened. Sabotage meant death not only for the guilty but for us all.

Although the department head (aided by an assistant) confessed to the theft, we acted as if we had no suspect. The culprit supported a wife and in-laws, but after what he did, I could not keep him in the Turnatoria. So I asked the mayor to assign him to the city water plant, where he worked until the liberation.

I have never understood how a man who held a diploma in mechanical engineering and spoke six languages could have committed such a crime. Two years later he had the courage to visit me in Bucharest. He asked for my forgiveness, telling me he must have been out of his mind to have done such a thing. I helped arrange his immigration to the United States but had nothing more to do with him.

*Commentary for*
*Part Four*

---

# Fall, 1942

THE AXIS armies reached the Volga River in early September, 1942, and joined the Battle of Stalingrad. The invaders began their encirclement of the city in mid-November, 1942, but failed to drive out the defending Soviet forces, which launched a decisive counteroffensive. After two additional months of combat in the frozen steppes of southern Russia and the loss of more than 150,000 men, German Field Marshal Friedrich Paulus capitulated. Hitler's generals also suffered defeat in North Africa.

The Nazis kept up their campaigns of genocide against Jews, Gypsies, Slavs, and other peoples they deemed inferior. It would be another eighteen months before the Soviets liberated the first death camp in Poland or the Western Allies landed at Normandy. Throughout the fall of 1942, deportations to killing centers from Nazi-dominated Europe and the massacres in occupied Soviet territories continued unchecked.

---

At the end of September, 1942, the German Railroad Administration scheduled the deportation of Romania's Jews to the Belzec death camp in Poland, oblivious to the fact that Bucharest had lost its initial ardor for the plan. On the Transnistria question, however, Marshal Antonescu stubbornly refused to end the purgatory of the exiles. On September 22, 1942, the Romanian government decreed the death penalty for any Jew beyond the age of fifteen caught crossing the Dniester back into Romania; persons abetting a Jewish fugitive risked up to twenty-five years at hard labor.

In November, 1942, Radu Lecca, general commissar for Jewish questions, called a meeting with members of the Jewish Center and Dr. Filderman to explore the possibility of evacuating the surviving Transnistria deportees to Palestine in exchange for an enormous ransom payment. The idea proved unfeasible but indicated that Antonescu—the man who once said, "I do not mind if history judges us barbarians"—had become mindful of historical retribution.

The efforts of Romanian officials to reduce the Jewish population in Moghilev through deprivation and the two massive evacuations to the death camps in Scazinet and Peciora (Peh-chee-oh-rah) proved unsuccessful; the number remained constant at about 15,000. Moghilev drew a constant stream of refugees from peripheral camps, where life was even more tenuous than in the city. In September, 1942, the gendarmerie had ordered the Jewish Committee to secure the Moghilev ghetto with barbed wire, but this too failed to slow the influx.

Jagendorf wrote little about the Peciora evacuations, which occurred during the tenure of Dr. Schauer. In October, 1942, three thousand Jews (including 600 locals) were evacuated by cattle car from Moghilev to Peciora. Living conditions were so deplorable in the desolate camp that the victims reportedly resorted to cannibalism.

One of the few Peciora survivors, Frida Koller, testified that Sergeant Hans Rucker, chief of a Nazi camp on the eastern bank of the Bug, had requisitioned from Peciora 150 Jewish women between the ages of fourteen and twenty. They were taken into a forest, raped, then shot. Five weeks later, another 500 Jews were taken over the Bug and executed. In less than one year, all but 28 of the 3,000 Jews sent to Peciora from Moghilev had perished.

Many Scazinet and Peciora evacuees chose to leave their children in Moghilev, where they felt the youngsters might have a better chance of survival. As a result, the number of known orphans in the colony rose to more than 500, requiring the establishment of a third orphanage on November 13, 1942. Food became so scarce during this period that the Jewish Committee was forced to close its soup kitchen and restrict the daily diet of each orphan to 100–150 grams of bread. In the month of November, 1942, sixty-two children died in the orphanages from malnutrition and disease.

Jagendorf reports that Schauer resigned as president because he was "weary of battling Jewish racketeers who conspired to seize control of the Jewish Committee." A letter cited by Shraga Yeshu-run in his study of the Jewish self-administration in the Moghilev ghetto shows that it was Jagendorf himself who had undermined Dr. Schauer. On October 19, 1942, Jagendorf asked Prefect Nat-uras to annul the Schauer committee, stating that "a number of members use their position to advance their commercial and pri-vate interests instead of caring for the well-being of the Jewish community as a whole." Jagendorf also alleged that the committee had lost the confidence of the Jews of Moghilev and of the Jewish Center in Bucharest.

On the question of distributing Jewish aid, Jagendorf wrote: "I have been ordered by the Jewish Center in Romania, as the man in whom they place their trust, to head all the assistance pro-grams in this district." According to Yeshurun, Jagendorf had based this claim on one sentence in a letter from the Jewish Cen-ter, dated September 9, 1942: "We have all hope that this im-portant project (referring specifically to orphan aid) will be done in the best way under the trustworthy leadership of Engineer Ja-gendorf. . . ." Jagendorf concluded his letter to Nasturas by re-questing permission to "organize, oversee, and coordinate all assistance work, without being an official member of the Jewish Committee of Moghilev."

Dr. Schauer resigned three weeks after Jagendorf's damaging letter to the prefect, leaving the committee without an official head from the first of November until mid-December, 1942, when Ja-gendorf began his second term.

-----

The Turnatoria families enjoyed a privileged status among Moghi-lev's Jews. They could expect a daily portion of bread and a bowl of soup, and, officially at least, were exempt from forced labor conscription and evacuation to the Lager. In gratitude to Jagendorf, the workers gathered in the Turnatoria on November 3, 1942, the first anniversary of the discovery of the factory, and presented their leader with a cigarette lighter and the following declaration:

"We first set foot in this foundry one year ago today. It's been only one year, Mr. Jagendorf, since you, with your ingenuity, sal-vaged a group of desperate people by giving us the opportunity to become both productive and self-sustaining, helping us forget our affliction.

"It has been a year filled with memories of all the hardships that you as director have endured. Out of chaos and destruction you created an atmosphere of respect for us, among those who have long forgotten what respect means. . . .

"It is with deep reverence and solemn silence that we remember the victims from our community who went to their eternal rest during the past year. . . .

"Those who have worked here from the beginning have enabled us to labor and to live in 'the ruins.' For all this and much more we are deeply thankful. . . . Your leadership and guidance have given us renewed strength to continue the enterprise that you so ably and courageously established."

As founding father of the Turnatoria, Siegfried Jagendorf demanded and received public tribute from his flock. He enjoyed his eminence and delighted in the laudatory verses of his courtier poetess, Paula Scharf. He required complete obeisance and tolerated no dissent.

Max Schmidt has unpleasant memories of Jagendorf's daily inspection tours.

"He said little to the engineers, except when he rebuked us in front of the workers. He refused to speak to the ordinary worker, who dared not address him, except through a predetermined intermediary. His message was unmistakable: 'I am in charge, and my word is law.' The workers feared Jagendorf, and out of this fear came their respect for him. To the outside world he was our leader. We, 'the little men,' worked very hard, not because he inspired us, but out of a determination to survive. Beyond that, we wanted to give him the power base he needed to deal forcefully with the authorities."

Jagendorf insisted that the state-owned factory not be exploited for personal profit. He feared that discovery of such abuses by the authorities would result in reprisals and termination of the Turnatoria as a Jewish-run operation. The workers, on the other hand, considered "doing business" necessary to supplement their grossly insufficient rations and to keep their families from starving to death. Turnatoria hands supplied the black market with horse-hair brushes, knives, cooking pots, cigarette lighters, and other modest utensils.

Michael Scherzer, a former toolmaker in the Turnatoria, recalled his quarrel with Jagendorf, when we met in a suburb of Haifa, Israel in August, 1989:

"To earn some extra money I joined two other workers who were fabricating and selling cigarette lighters. Jagendorf discovered our little operation and expelled us from the factory, though thankfully not from the housing complex. We pleaded with him for three months before he finally pardoned us, probably because he needed toolmakers."

Herman Sattinger, who now lives in Brooklyn, New York, found a haven in the Jagendorf's Turnatoria during the war. The former foundry specialist smiled as he related how he had produced aluminum pots for cooking mamaliga (a porridge of cornmeal popular in Romania) and bartered them for food. One day the Turnatoria detective (also named Sattinger but no relation) caught him leaving the grounds with one of the pots under his shirt. The foundry worker was told that a report would be filed with Jagendorf, who certainly would expel him from the Turnatoria community. The threat proved groundless. After a while, aluminum pots reappeared in the market place.

The workers regularly pilfered supplies from the Turnatoria. Jacob Vogel of Cleveland, Ohio, recounted in a telephone interview how one snowy day a crowd of Turnatoria workers about to break for lunch received word of an impending gate search. "Everyone reached into their clothes and unloaded handfuls of wood, coal, and other materials. In an instant, a large pile of contraband darkened the ground. They never checked us again; rather, as we passed by, the guard would observe, 'You look like you had a big breakfast this morning.' "

Theft in the Turnatoria was a fact of life that no amount of intimidation could deter. "That the workers defied him," commented Max Schmidt, "proves that the need to eat is stronger than the fear of punishment." Schmidt added:

"Jagendorf often ordered the fabrication of cigarette lighters to be used by him in his dealings with the authorities; it was only natural for the workers to produce a surplus of lighters for their own purposes. When Jagendorf found out, he took me to task for not properly supervising my department. I pointed that they want to eat and I cannot wean them of that habit.

"My colleague Engineer Leo Litmann of the foundry department acted as I did; he knew what the workers were doing but did not interfere. Jagendorf chastised Litmann from the foundry doorway because the director did not want to risk tripping on the castings and soil his clothes. Engineers Morgenstern, Rauch, and Brandman all protected their workers and often were scolded harshly by Jagendorf. None of us wanted to harm Jagendorf or the Turnatoria. Inasmuch as we knew of no complaints or threats leveled against our director by the Romanian authorities, we regarded his uncompromising stance as an unwarranted and overzealous intrusion."

In mid-January, 1943, thirteen members of the Turnatoria's leadership joined forces in calling on Jagendorf to pardon all workers who had abused factory privileges. Their letter recommended the creation of two workers' courts, one to judge violations by ordinary workers and a second to rule on the misdeeds of managers. These courts, the letter added, "should consist of unprejudiced, objective people and be given the power of enforcement. . . ." Although Jagendorf remained adamant in demanding of employees higher standards of ethical conduct than would be required in normal times, he acceded to the letter's recommendations, which signaled unanimous internal disapproval of the director's disciplinary excesses.

In the curious episode of the stolen transmission belt, Jagendorf indirectly accused Max Schmidt and an accomplice of sabotage. Forty-six years later in New York, I asked Mr. Schmidt about the incident. Shocked by accusation, Max Schmidt denied angrily that the belt had been removed and accused Jagendorf of inventing the episode for the purpose of self-aggrandizement:

"The raised belt was about 180 feet long and weighed about 200 pounds. To lower it with two men would have been impossible, and to conceal such an operation from the factory guards and from the ever-vigilant Popescu (the government overseer) would have been inconceivable. And where in Moghilev could Pinkas Katz have found a temporary replacement belt of such dimensions? The belt never was removed, only a length of about four feet once had to be trimmed off to adjust for slack. Some of the workers, I believe, cut the remnant into pieces and made soles for their shoes. That was no crime."

Schmidt's defense is difficult to dispute. Other former Turnatoria workers I interviewed had no recollection of the alleged crime. Why would Jagendorf want to discredit Schmidt, his technical adviser from the very first day in the Turnatoria? Perhaps the motive was professional jealousy. Jagendorf was the only Turnatoria engineer who lacked a university diploma, a deficiency he kept strictly secret. Everyone assumed that he had received the highest level of professional training because of his much flaunted association with Siemens-Schukert Werke, even though he had left that company eighteen years before the deportation. Jagendorf erected a social barrier between himself and the other Jewish engineers in the Turnatoria, avoiding personal and even technical discussions. Max Schmidt recalled:

"My colleagues and I worked harmoniously, helping each other solve engineering problems. We never could get any specific advice from our chief, Engineer Jagendorf. When he found it necessary to tell a German or Romanian officer whether or not the Turnatoria could handle a particular job, he never committed himself without first consulting one of us."

As the dominant engineer in Moghilev, Jagendorf took credit for repairing the damaged power plant. Schmidt told me that it was Engineer Bruno Brandman, former manager of the Cernauti power plant, who led the crew that repaired the power station in Moghilev, the achievement that made Jagendorf, "the talk of the town." Jagendorf makes no reference to Engineer Brandman, whom he disliked.

Mechanical Engineers Schmidt (lathe and power plant department) and Joseph Morgenstern (locksmithing department) and Bruno Brandman received their engineering diplomas from the German Technical University in Brno, Czechoslovakia. Engineer Rauch (punchpress and toolshop department) graduated from the Sorbonne; and Engineers Litmann (foundry and casting department) and Pincu Melman (drafting) graduated from the Technical University in Bucharest.

Jagendorf acknowledged the contributions of only a handful of associates, not one of them an engineer. He mentions "Architect Samuel Kurzweil . . . who restored the factory buildings"; "Mr. Max Heissman . . . a dedicated administrator who spoke all the languages of the workers"; "Dr. Hillel Brender . . . an attorney who advised me on financial questions"; "Dr. Jonas Kessler . . . an attorney who counseled me on political matters and ran the department of social welfare"; "Mr. David Rennert . . . a man who knew how to get along with all the officials in procuring food for us"; "Mr. Isidor Pressner . . . who ran the foodstores and kitchen"; and "Hermann Metsch . . . who grew fresh vegetables for the orphans."

*Part Five*

---

# WINTER, 1942–1943

**DEATH WAGON**
*Jagendorf Archives, Yad Vashem, The Holocaust Martyrs' and Heroes'
Remembrance Authority, Jerusalem*

# 1

## SAVING THE ORPHANS

O<small>NE</small> <small>DAY</small> in early winter, 1942–1943, the Turnatoria received a camera for repair, providing an opportunity to photograph our emaciated orphans and smuggle the film to Bucharest with an appeal for help.

The doctors of our three orphanages had just issued an alarming report stating that about one-third of the 659 children must be considered terminally ill. The cemetery department reported that from October to mid-December, 1942, ninety-three children had died in our orphanages. In addition, many unprotected children had perished on the streets.

I showed the findings to Dr. Meyer Weinstein, a prominent pediatrician who served as the Turnatoria doctor. He examined all the children in our orphanages and found that even the sickest among them could be saved if immediately administered a special diet. I approved the doctor's proposal and ordered the orphanages to procure the necessary food, regardless of cost. We emptied a large room in one of our hospitals, where groups of fifty children were rehabilitated in two-week rotations. All of the children survived.

Housing the orphans was difficult because city officials frequently confiscated the buildings after we had renovated them.

We also lacked the wood to build beds, tables, chairs, and other furnishings. This sad situation improved dramatically after we received a carload of lumber from the Jewish Center in Bucharest. Later, we acquired books and writing materials for use in the orphan house. We fabricated toys, dishes, spoons, and other useful items in the Turnatoria. The following letter was sent to Mrs. Jagendorf from the directors of Orphanage #1:

". . . In the name of the interned children, many thanks for having brought them twenty toys. We take this opportunity also to express our gratitude for your personal interest in the well-being of these children. Our most difficult task is to dispel the terrible images that plague these little souls who witnessed the tragic fate of their parents.

"Please accept our gratitude for your sincere expressions of consolation. When the children someday write your praises, the words will be composed with gold letters. But in the meantime, you can see it in their bright and thankful eyes. We hope you will favor us with a visit soon."

The orphanage directors produced plays, using the children as actors. Orphans wrote, edited, and produced a bimonthly newspaper called *Gazeta Sperantei* (Newspaper of Hope). Our house poet, Miss Paula Scharf, dedicated to Mrs. Jagendorf the following poem entitled "Prayers of the Orphan Children":

*Found on all the streets,*
*Nobody to watch us.*
*By begging we live*
*One giving, another not.*

*Alone in this world,*
*Parents dead,*
*Driven from house and courtyard.*
*Into an orphanage.*

*The first night, lying in bed,*
*Pictures of days long ago,*
*Mother kissing us good night,*
*Breakfast of bread and butter.*

*Home now is a hard bed,*
*The longing and tears we choke.*
*Life forges us into hard steel.*
*The sun no longer shines.*

*Outside snow whirls, white flakes.*
*We must stay in bed.*
*One of us looks through the window,*
*How we envy the children at play.*

*Suddenly it is quiet,*
*One hears a gentle rustle.*
*Our eyes fix on the door.*
*A fairy appears, bearing baskets of food.*

*She walks to each bed, strokes our hair.*
*Eyes shine, bright and happy*
*Soothe our sorrow, good fairy,*
*In chorus, we thank the Lord.*

# 2

---

# THE SARAGA
# COMMISSION

The Turnatoria now employed about 700 workers in three shifts. The first group of apprentices entered the work force, allowing new cadets to enroll in our technical studies program.

Just before Christmas, 1942, the state police commander called me to his home and informed me that a five-person Jewish commission from Bucharest made up of Jews and a senior government official would soon arrive in Moghilev. I had no prior knowledge of the visit.

Several days later, a sergeant summoned me to police headquarters, where I met Mr. Fred Saraga and his delegation, which had come to determine what aid we needed. They ate and slept at the police station, and their movements were closely monitored. Nevertheless, I found a way to talk with Mr. Saraga in private. He told me that Governor Alexianu had praised our work in Moghilev, simplifying the commission's relief efforts.

"How is it," I asked, "that a Jewish delegation was allowed to come here?"

"Marshall Antonescu wanted to speak to a Jewish leader regarding certain matters. The governor recommended that you be brought to Bucharest. I thought it would be much better if we came here to see you."

To determine our specific needs, the delegation visited the Turnatoria, shops, orphanages, and other institutions. Before leaving to inspect another camp, Mr. Saraga promised his unswerving support. Subsequently, the Bucharest pipeline flowed more generously.

# 3

---

# "ROAR OF THE TURNATORIA"

O<small>N THE</small> evening of January 28, 1943, my co–workers presented me with a book commemorating the first anniversary of my beating. Entitled "The Roar of the Turnatoria," it opened with the following dedication:

"Siegfried Jagendorf. Today marks the anniversary of the day that you assumed full responsibility for us. You had the courage to snatch another Jew from their hands and bear the brunt of their rage. They hurled you to the ground, tortured, and humiliated you. . . . Another would have perished, but you bore your blows proudly, with honor . . . Your name will be remembered always. . . ."

The book's contents included poems and caricatures of the factory leadership by a talented young man named S. Eisinger. My portrait carried the caption: "A whole man is standing in front of you. He created lives from ruins."

Max Heissman, my secretary, contributed the following vision of how posterity might record our presence in Moghilev:

"Five hundred years ago, a time before people knew peace or equality of race and religion, a great many Jews, as they were called then, were deported to a place called Transnistria, across the Dniester River in the eastern region of Pan-Europe. In that time of war, the Turnatoria produced goods to benefit mankind. . . .

"Only a small number of those Jews survived the cold, hunger, and typhus—a terrible sickness unknown today. A number of Jews remained in Moghilev–Podolski, a city today inhabited by millions but a small town then. Most of them engaged in commerce, but a small group led by a man with great vision, an energetic organizer, rebuilt a big machine factory which had been destroyed in the war. They did so despite the terrible cold, hunger, and even without the primitive tools then in use. The original plant has been preserved by the government as a museum where visitors view the primitive diesel motor that powered the plant. Management insisted on the principle of absolute honesty. Workers were expected to forgo personal benefit for the sake of the common good.

"A few people did not embrace these principles, choosing the wickedness of the black market. They profiteered on the backs of the sick and dying, selling sacred medicine at extortionate prices. Our leader, honest and dedicated to his unfortunate co–workers, detested these machinations. One day, he discovered the deception, how some conducted their dirty business under the cover of his good name. The unclean were eliminated, while those faithful to the cause and to him made history.

"Our leader lived to tell the tale and received his due recognition and reward. In the museum one can view the old machines, read the old chronicles, and give tribute to the great man and his group, who, despite the great danger and deprivation, chose the path of honesty."

# 4

---

# GOOD GERMANS

$S$OME GERMANS disagreed privately with Hitler's policies and helped us whenever possible. One such person was the commander of a large hospital in Moghilev. He frequently came to us for technical assistance, and we always obliged. One Sunday a Jewish patient needing surgery arrived in Moghilev from a nearby Lager. Our doctors informed me that they lacked the necessary instruments and drugs. I phoned the German hospital commander. Within minutes he and his chief surgeon came to Turnatoria to discuss the case with our hospital head. They agreed on the diagnosis and later performed the operation jointly, saving the patient.

On another occasion, I asked the hospital commander for the loan of an ambulance.

"You need it for a Jew, I presume."

"Yes," I replied.

"I could face the noose, if they find out that the patient is a Jew. I'll simply hide that fact." The plan worked.

A unit of the Todt group [the Nazi organization for large-scale construction work] arrived in Moghilev to build a bridge over the Dniester. The captain in charge visited me in the Turnatoria and requested some technical advice. Then he said, "I suppose you are worried about our using your people on the project. I assure you that no harm will come to any Jew working for me. Should you have any trouble, call on me any time." I did have to call him once, after a Jewish worker had been shot dead at the work site. The captain apologized and reprimanded the guilty soldier. The bridge was completed without further bloodshed.

*Commentary for*
*Part Five*

---

# Winter, 1942–43

THE SOVIETS launched three major offensives in winter, 1942–43. In North Africa, British troops entered Tripoli at the end of January. In the Pacific, U.S. forces drove the Japanese from Guadalcanal in early February. The contemporaneous but far-flung battles of Stalingrad, El Alamein, and Guadalcanal turned the tide irreversibly in favor of the Allies.

In the war against Europe's Jews, deportations to extermination centers continued—Polish Jews to Belzec and Treblinka, the Jews of western Europe (also the Gypsies) to Auschwitz–Birkenau. In the occupied areas of the Soviet Union, mobile killing squads pursued their genocidal aims.

---

On December 10, 1942, the Queen Mother Helena informed Marshal Antonescu that she did not want her son's name (King Michael) associated with Romania's anti-Jewish persecutions. Two days later, the German ambassador to Romania, Manfred von Killinger reported to the Foreign Office in Berlin that Marshal Antonescu was considering a plan to send 75,000–80,000 Jews to Palestine for a $107 million ransom payment. The Germans took strong exception to the scheme, which, in any event, had little practical significance because of the overwhelming obstacles to shipping Jews safely from Romania to the Middle East in wartime, and because London had closed Palestine to Jewish immigration. The futility of escape had been dramatized tragically the previous winter, when an old cattle boat called the *Struma*, carrying 769 Jews from Romania, sank off the Turkish coast after being torpedoed, probably by a Soviet submarine that mistook the vessel for an enemy ship. The disaster could have been averted had the Turkish or British governments given the refugees sanctuary.

---

On December 15, 1942, as the exiles settled into their second winter in Transnistria, Jagendorf began his final term as chief of Moghilev's Jews, setting as his top priorities the prevention of another epidemic and the rehabilitation of the orphans. Neither the Romanian authorities nor the Jewish Center in Bucharest provided assistance.

Jagendorf wrote to the Jewish Center, complaining that it had asked him to establish a district orphanage in Moghilev for 1,000 orphans but failed to send the promised funding. He said that the transfer of the children had to be delayed until all "necessary measures" were taken, especially because the conditions in the three orphanages in Moghilev were already "catastrophic."

At the end of December, 1942, Jagendorf received the findings of an internal report on conditions in Moghilev's three Jewish orphanages. Of a total of 679 children, 84 were between the ages of one and six, 386 between the ages of seven and thirteen, and 209 between the ages of fourteen and twenty. Almost one-third of the children were in danger of dying from malnutrition. The most prevalent disease was scabies, a contagious and itchy skin disease caused by a parasitic mite. Most of the children had to remain in bed all day because they had no clothes; as a result of inactivity, their joints grew stiff and their muscles wasted away. The report recommended that the children be given clothes, even if only made of straw, to enable them to move about in their dormitories. The report also recommended moving the healthy children in the oldest group to a separate building, where they could get job training; moving the sick children to a special care unit, where they could receive better food; acquiring lumber to build beds; and dismissing gratuitous personnel. Jagendorf wrote on the corner of the report, "I agree with the memo, especially with the way it should be handled."

The day after receiving the report, Jagendorf applied to the mayor of Moghilev for the use of two buildings to house the orphans. With respect to a specific school building, Jagendorf wrote, "I want to underscore that School No. 3 had been rented to us but we were obliged to evacuate the facility because of its proximity to some military barracks. I am sure that you will demonstrate your concern for the orphans by agreeing to shelter in a humane manner the unhappiest of all the unhappy people."

On January 2, 1943, Dr. Wilhelm Filderman, having been apprised of the conditions by Jewish leaders in Transnistria and armed with photos of the emaciated youngsters, wrote the first of many appeals to Mihai and Ion Antonescu on behalf of the orphans. He informed them: "In one orphanage with 140 children, 26 have died in one month. They are naked, sleeping on beds without sheets, in unheated rooms without window panes, unable to get out of bed. . . ." He made one recommendation: "Return the children under eighteen immediately to Cernauti, where living costs are a quarter of what they are in Transnistria, and where public charity can provide food and care."

The German exerted heavy pressure on the Romanian government not to bring back the orphans. It would take another thirteen months before Antonescu finally allowed their repatriation.

The Jewish Center made its first on-site inspection of the deportees on January 6, 1943, when Fred Saraga (Shah-rah-gah), a Jewish official from Iasi, led a four-member commission to study Jewish conditions in Transnistria. The Saraga Commission found that three-quarters of the Jewish children deported from Transnistria had died. Of the surviving youths, about 8,000 had lost one or both parents. Saraga devoted himself to the repatriation of these children, who referred to him as "the father of the orphans" and composed songs in his honor.

In reporting his conversation with Fred Saraga, Jagendorf recalled the envoy's saying that Marshal Antonescu had wanted to speak with a deported Jewish leader and that Governor Alexianu had recommended Jagendorf be brought to Bucharest for this purpose. It is highly unlikely that Antonescu would have proposed summoning a Jew from Transnistria for a consultation. Fred Saraga's writings do not substantiate Jagendorf's interpretation.

According to Dr. Ben-Zion, fourteen orphanages had been established by local Jewish committees in Transnistria, providing 1,842 children with minimal food, clothing, and medical care. Funding came primarily from clandestine Jewish relief organizations and private contributors in Romania. Prior to the establishment of the orphanages, the children had to either beg, scavenge, or steal their food. When the first typhus epidemic broke out, the filthy young vagabonds became pariahs, blamed for spreading the disease. The orphanages became a necessity both to save and to quarantine these unfortunate children.

The following poem, composed in Yiddish by Relly Blei, was given to me in Israel by Meir Shefi, head of the organization of Transnistria orphans:

## The Wandering Orphans

### Moghilev, 1943

*The orphans wander, driven by hunger*
*They beg at doors: "a piece of bread, please!"*
*Angry, you refuse to open.*
*Not wanting to see.*

*The days are rushing, the months dashing.*
*Winter is cold, the hunger hurts.*
*In the streets, children fall frozen.*
*Passing, you avert your eyes.*

*Still they wander, driven by hunger.*
*"Have pity, a piece of bread, please."*
*You bolt your heart,*
*Leaving them in the grip of death.*

*People, open your eyes.*
*That's not vermin and lice*
*That's the wandering seed of your brother,*
*His child!*

*You help the enemy, don't you see,*
*When you close your doors and hearts*
*To the children who plead,*
*"A piece of bread, please."*

Many orphans had to struggle on their own, as did thirteen-year-old Fanny Rosen, who was deported with her family to Transnistria from Cernauti in the fall of 1941. Mrs. Rosen recounted her ordeal in a letter to me:

"From Moghilev we walked two weeks until we reached our destination, the Lager Grabifti. The Ukrainians and Romanian guards pointed to an empty barn and told us and several other families that this would be our home now. Every able-bodied man had to labor in the forest, felling trees or doing some other back-breaking work. My father, a pious Jew and no longer a young man, often failed to meet his quota and returned from work empty-handed. When he did bring home a ration, he gave me the largest portion so that I might live.

"One day, German soldiers entered the camp and told us to form a line and to keep our mouths shut. When they demanded money and jewelry from everyone, my mother became fearful. My father tried to calm her. He whispered something in her ear. A German ordered him to step forward, and, without a word, shot him. He who had brought us the meager ration was dead.

"The next day, I slipped out of the camp to find something to eat. I collected a bowl full of snails and frogs from a nearby pond and brought the catch home to cook and share with my mother, who was getting weaker and weaker. She soon died of starvation. Sometimes I was caught and beaten by the Jewish police and sometimes by Ukrainians, who scarred my back for life with their whips.

"One day, I overheard people planning an escape. I joined them, but we were caught. The guards shot several of the adults. I was fourteen but looked eight, just skin and bones. They took me to a barn, where they beat and gang raped me. They left me to die. After some time, an old woman helped me to my feet and advised me to escape as soon as I could walk. The guards would not miss me because they thought I was dead.

"That night, I crawled to the village and knocked on the first door in sight. A Ukrainian woman peered at me as if I had dropped down from another planet. My lice-infested body was caked in blood and filth. She asked me what I wanted. Food, I told her. She took me to the barn and asked what jobs I could do. Knitting, I replied. She said I could stay as long as I worked for my keep. Then she washed me and brought out some food. The next day she provided a ball of home-spun wool and told me to knit a pair of mittens. The Germans demanded that each household meet a quota of mittens, shawls, sweaters, or socks. I thanked my mother, may her name be blessed, for having taught me how to knit.

"After the Russians recaptured the area, I heard that all orphans were being organized for immigration to Palestine. I made my way to the city of Moghilev, where I told Jewish officials that I was an orphan and wanted to join my relatives in Palestine. They rejected my application, informing me that I was too old—three months too old. I was devastated. I discovered later that one of the members of the orphan committee had put his daughter on the list in my place."

---

When typhus struck again in winter, 1942–1943, the cynical Romanian authorities attributed the epidemic to Jewish unpreparedness and refused to provide assistance. The Jewish committees in Transnistria had taken steps to improve sanitation but still lacked the proper disinfection apparatus and medicine. Jagendorf wrote dozens of letters to the prefect, gendarme commander, and mayor requesting rations, medicine, soap, and other supplies. All his appeals were denied.

On December 31, 1942, Jagendorf petitioned Major Botoroaga (the third gendarme commander) for authorizations to transfer three doctors to Moghilev from district Lager to help organize a ghetto sanitation program. The commander scrawled in the margin, "There are already too many doctors in Moghilev, so I do not consider it necessary to approve your request. You are responsible for the new epidemic because you did not organize effectively. . . ."

At a meeting of Jewish doctors in Moghilev on January 10, 1943, a top Romanian medical officer announced, "We sent you here to die, but we bid you to stop the epidemic." Two days later, the prefecture's sanitation director, Dr. Liviu Marcu, complained to the Jewish Committee about the inadequate performance of Jewish doctors in preventing the spread of the typhus epidemic. Medical relief did not materialize until March, 1943, when the Jewish Center's shipment of antityphus serum reached Moghilev from Bucharest after many delays.

The principal conduit for clandestine aid to Transnistria was the Jewish Council in Bucharest, a secret coalition of Jewish leaders led by Dr. Filderman, Chief Rabbi Safran, Misu Benvenisti and Wilhelm Fischer (of the Zionist Organization), Fery Froimescu (of the Sephardic communities), and attorney Arnold Schwefelberg. The Jewish Council maintained contacts with the International Red Cross and the World Jewish Congress.

Vital underground relief was also provided by the Vaad Ezra V'hatzlah (the Zionist aid and rescue committee); a Hassidic organization in Cernauti led by the Sekulener Rebbe, Alexander Zusha Portugal; a group associated with Traian Popovici, the deposed (non-Jewish) mayor of Cernauti; the American Joint Distribution Committee, and from private individuals via couriers.

Much of the aid from the Jewish Center did not reach the intended recipients or arrived late due to bureaucratic obstacles by Romanian agencies and banks, poor communication, and arbitrary distribution channels to the remote camps. Corruption in Transnistria involving officials and their Jewish accomplices further undermined rescue efforts.

Max Schmidt told me that he and the other Turnatoria workers received no compensation beyond their daily portion of bread and soup:

"We benefited neither from outside aid nor from our own productivity. The Turnatoria supposedly received produce from the farms in payment for our manufactured goods and services, but we never saw any vegetables or fruits. On one occasion the factory received a large drum of cooking oil from a farm as payment for tractor parts. We were told that the delivery had been a mistake, and the drum disappeared. It resurfaced a few days later on the black market. That's how we discovered the existence of a cabal involving several top Turnatoria people and the prefect. There was a double standard: Jagendorf penalized the little people for using the factory to make objects for sale, but he tolerated the powerful clique that made off with communal provisions."

Schmidt believes that Jagendorf kept clean, with the possible exception of accepting personal gifts from the profiteers: "It was not unusual for Jagendorf to arrive at the Turnatoria wearing an expensive new hat or jacket. Everyday at lunchtime he would walk to his house and sit down to a good meal, served to him by his wife and the other women in the household." By all accounts, except his own, Jagendorf maintained a superior standard of living in Moghilev; however, he refused to exploit his privileged position for financial gain, projecting himself as a paragon of virtue against a background of villainy.

———

During his second term, Jagendorf intensified the campaign to root out petty corruption in Moghilev's Jewish institutions. On December 23, 1942, he received the findings of a special commission investigating conditions in the hospital for contagious diseases. It concluded that of the eighty person staff, thirty-three were not needed. Eight people lived in the hospital illicitly, including the pharmacist and three members of his family. The facility's record-keeping was slipshod. The report cited one case in which two pillows and a blanket were "lent" to a woman "with the approval of the hospital director and with the knowledge of Engineer Jagendorf." The report recommended dismissal of the hospital director for gross mismanagement. An investigation of the outpatient clinic revealed similar problems: excessive staff, nepotism, improper bookkeeping, and unchecked theft of food and bedding.

On January 25, 1943, an investigation of the local Jewish labor office showed that its director, Mihail Danilof, arbitrarily lowered the taxes of certain individuals and fully exempted others, including himself.

Jagendorf contested any Jewish rival who sought to establish an independent power base in Moghilev. On February 16, 1943, for instance, he secured the prefect's approval to oust Architect Donnenfeld as director of the city's Jewish communal trade shops. Donnenfeld complained to Dr. Filderman, accusing his "co-nationals" of sabotaging enterprises under his control and preventing him from becoming president of the committee, even though he had Major Botoroaga's backing. Moses Katz defended Jagendorf's action, informing Filderman in a secret memorandum that Donnenfeld and Danilof had engaged in influence peddling, embezzlement, and black marketeering. The Soviets later arrested Donnenfeld on suspicion of collaboration with the enemy; he reportedly died in prison.

On January 28, 1943, the first anniversary of Jagendorf's beating, a group of Turnatoria workers published a satirical newspaper containing poems, a play, a cautionary tale, essays, and caricatures of the foundry's leading figures. The publication portrayed Jagendorf reverentially. His caricature, for example, carried the caption, "A whole man stands before you. He created life from ruins." There was little evidence of nobility in the portraits of the other factory personalities, whose foibles were mocked by the talented young draftsman, S. Eisinger. The purpose of the commemorative newspaper, according to its editors, was to "put a little smile on

grieved faces and to blunt our common distress with a bit of cheer-
fullness.''

———————————

Jagendorf indicates that his main contacts with Germans in Moghilev were with military men who requisitioned Jewish labor or requested special favors, such as watch repairs, precision engraving,
or jewelry making. The committee president did not encounter the
brutal killing units staffed by ethnic Germans (*Volksdeutche*), who
completed their dirty work in the area and moved eastward before
Jagendorf's arrival in Transnistria.

Jagendorf found it difficult to accept the moral failings of a cul-
ture with which he had so fervently identified. He seems to have
believed, naively, that the Germans had erred in persecuting the
Jews. If only the true value of Jewish ingenuity and industriousness
could be demonstrated, as in the Turnatoria, the Germans and
Romanians alike would recognize the shortsightedness of their
anti-Semitic policies. Jagendorf subscribed to no particular political ideology, but he held firmly to the Jewish Enlightenment view
that a thorough secular education could redeem the superstitious
ghetto Jew of Europe and usher him into the twentieth century as
a productive member of society. This may explain Jagendorf's emphasis on technical training for Jewish youth. (From 1935–1940,
he had served on the faculty of the ORT Jewish technical school in
Cernauti.) Many of the youths who trained in the Turnatoria apprenticeship program, including Jagendorf's nephew Adalbert Regenstreif, went on to become accomplished engineers in Israel and
in the United States.

*Part Six*

---

# SPRING–SUMMER, 1943

# 1

# CHANGING OF THE GUARD

Major Romeo Orasanu, commander of the legion of gendarmes in Moghilev, was transferred in April, 1943. He had been unsympathetic but susceptible to pressure and persuasion because of his personal doubts about an ultimate Nazi victory. When Major Orasanu introduced me to his successor, Major Gheorghe Botoroaga, I asked the new commander if his brother was an engineer. He said yes and asked me how I knew him. I replied that I had hired Engineer Botoroaga for a position at Siemens–Schukert Werke. The coincidence made no impression on this cruel man.

Major Botoroaga had acted indecently when he served as gendarme commander during the brutal deportations from Suceava, and he behaved no better in Moghilev. I assigned one of our spies to record the commander's moves, both in the gendarmerie and in its adjoining courtroom. The major rarely bothered to bring arrested Jews to trial, even though he presided as the judge. After beating prisoners, he sometimes ordered their execution, simply writing "EX" on the files.

Whenever I learned of an arrest, I rushed to the gendarmerie and asked to see the charge sheet, obliging the major to comply with judicial procedures. The commander acted cautiously in my presence, having been briefed about my powerful connections in Bucharest. He was always looking for bribes, using his wife as an intermediary. I neither paid nor accepted bribes, but sometimes advised hostages to satisfy the major's demands in order to save themselves. In such cases, my direct intervention would have been counterproductive. The major and I adopted a stance of civility, careful to avoid a clash.

We would lose Colonel Nasturas as well. He informed me that he had been ordered to change places with the prefect of Tulcin, Colonel Constantin Loghin. Compared to Loghin, Nasturas was a saint. The district of Tulcin was practically purged of Jews as a result of Colonel Loghin's enthusiasm for dispatching our people to the German exterminators across the Bug. It was he who had sent 3,000 Jews to their deaths the previous summer, when only the Costiner family survived.

We received two important visitors in the final days of Colonel Nasturas' tenure. In April, 1943, while inspecting the Turnatoria departments, I learned that the prefect and an entourage of about fifty under-secretaries and secret servicemen were waiting for me in the yard. When I arrived, Colonel Nasturas introduced me to Mr. Busila, the secretary of transportation and communication. The official greeted me with an embrace. "We know each other," he said, "what are you doing here?" "I am a Jew," I replied. Mr. Busila and I had worked together as Siemens–Schukert directors. He asked me to accompany him back to Bucharest. "Not alone," I answered. "Of course, with your family," he said. "No, Mr. Secretary, I mean with all the Jews here, especially the orphaned children. Should I now save my life and abandon them?" "I understand you perfectly," he said, "but it is not in my power to take all of them back, only you and your family." As we walked through the factory, he tried to convince me to change my mind. Colonel Nasturas also tried to persuade me to accept Mr. Busila's invitation, warning that life under Colonel Loghin would be terrible. He refused even to speak to a Jew. I held to my decision. Secretary Busila's offer to repatriate me reinforced the perception among local officials that I had friends in the highest places.

# 2

# THE BRIBE

ONE DAY, a man entered my office and handed me a letter confirming his appointment as the government commissar of the Turnatoria. I saw no reason to oppose the order, even if I could; perhaps Engineer Eugen Popescu could help us cut through governmental red tape. But why had an official watchdog been installed in the Turnatoria? Colonel Nasturas didn't know.

In March, 1943, Transnistria's director of industry, Ion Fotiade, a former leader of the violently anti-Semitic Iron Guard, arrived in Moghilev to inspect the Turnatoria. I put the workers on full alert, anticipating a bitter struggle. Mr. Fotiade greeted me cordially and asked for a tour of the plant. Observing the workers engaged in difficult jobs, he questioned me about their backgrounds. He could hardly believe that the young women working in the foundry department had received their training in our technical school. Organizational efficiency such as ours could be found only in the most highly developed industrial countries. I showed him a stack of new orders for parts and requested the necessary raw materials, particularly coke for the foundry. He promised to send the supplies. When I brought up the question of bread rations owed us, he said the matter was out of his hands.

Mr. Fotiade called for an increase in the production of tractor parts and nails, stipulated that the necessary transmission belts be furnished by the government, and ordered us to store the coke more securely. He reaffirmed my position as director but retained Commissar Popescu, giving him veto power over my decisions. Disputes over factory policy would be mediated by the prefect, technical questions by Mr. Fotiade. I was heartened by Mr. Fotiade's report but distressed that the hateful Popescu, who knew nothing about engineering or plant management, could go on using his position to harass me and to fill his bottomless pockets.

During Mr. Fotiade's inspection of the Turnatoria, I was approached by Mihail Danilof, director of our labor coordinating office. He informed me that an influential sub-director of Transnistria's department of finance, Mr. Alexandru Tugui, had arrived in Moghilev with orders to assess our activities.

Mr. Danilof wanted me to authorize a bribe requested by Mr. Tugui in payment for a positive report. I refused, warning him to stay clear of such business. I suspected a plot against Mr. Danilof, who previously had been involved with officials in dirty dealings. The next day Mr. Danilof wanted to see me again, but I was busy with Mr. Fotiade. I asked Mr. Isidor Pressner, who was in charge of finances, to reiterate my absolute opposition to the bribe. But Danilof convinced Pressner to give him 20,000 lei [$100] to pay off Tugui.

The next day, Major Botoroaga summoned Pressner, Danilof, and me to the gendarmerie. I sent a message explaining that a meeting with Mr. Fotiade precluded my coming, but that I would send the other two. I learned the next day that Mr. Tugui had reported the payoff to Commander Botoroaga, who promptly arrested and beat Mr. Danilof. I hurried to the gendarmerie, where I was told that Mr. Danilof had signed a deposition asserting that the Jewish Committee had authorized the bribe. Danilof's treachery had imperiled the entire colony.

I asked the investigating officer, a decent man and a friend, to question the prisoner in my presence. Danilof was brought in and confessed that he had acted against my order. When I questioned his judgment as an attorney and leader, he replied that he must have been out of his mind. I pleaded with the officer to intercede. He said Mr. Tugui had left Moghilev and surely would report the incident to Governor Alexianu. He had no choice but to notify the military court in Tiraspol.

A few days later, the prefect informed me that in reaction to Mr. Tugui's report the governor had ordered the Jewish Committee of Moghilev to be interned at Vapniarca, a notorious Lager for Jewish political prisoners. The arrest order noted that I was to be exempted from punishment.

I dispatched a courier to Bucharest, requesting that an attorney be sent to Tiraspol. Then I returned to the gendarmerie and received Major Botoroaga's pledge not to transfer the detainees to Vapniarca before the military tribunal had reached its verdict.

On May 11, 1943, thirteen of us boarded a heavily-guarded train for the overnight trip to Tiraspol. Upon arrival, Danilof and Pressner were jailed and the rest of us quartered in a compound occupied by about one hundred Jewish tradespeople. We did not meet the defense attorney until the morning of the trial. On the witness stand, I testified that neither Danilof nor Pressner had the right to speak in the name of the Jewish Committee or to allocate funds. Such functions were the prerogative of the president alone, and I had specifically disapproved of the payment. I questioned why Mr. Tugui had bypassed me and solicited money from Mr. Danilof. After hearing the testimony, including Mr. Tugui's, the tribunal deliberated for an hour before returning a not-guilty verdict. Danilof and Pressner accompanied us back to Moghilev.

Upon our return, we learned that Major Botoroaga had ordered the arrest of my four committee members, who were to be transfered immediately to Vapniarca. The mean-spirited gendarme commander did not regard acquittal as sufficient cause to dismiss the pretrial arrest warrants. The fight to redeem Mihail Danilof, Isidor Pressner, Jonas Kessler, and Josef Laufer would have to be waged during the tenure of Moghilev's third prefect, Colonel Constantin Loghin.

# 3

---

# LOGHIN THE TERRIBLE

As his first official act, Colonel Constantin Loghin assembled all prefectura personnel and asked: "Do you have a dominant Jew here?"

"Yes," replied Engineer Popescu, "Jew Jagendorf, director of the Turnatoria."

"Fire him!" proclaimed the prefect.

Colonel Loghin then bragged about kicking out a Jew within five minutes of taking office. Engineer Popescu neglected to tell the colonel that firing me exceeded the prefect's authority. The Turnatoria was now under the jurisdiction of the minister of industry in Odessa, who had appointed me district chief of the newly created central Jewish labor office.

When Mr. Popescu informed me of my dismissal, I requested a written order. He refused and wired Mr. Ion Fotiade for a ruling: "The Prefect ordered me to fire Engineer Jagendorf as director of the Turnatoria and replace him with a Ukrainian. How shall I handle it?" Mr. Fotiade replied: "I do not approve of any change in the management of the Turnatoria. Report immediately in writing on the situation. What provoked the intervention?"

Colonel Loghin revoked his dismissal order and never again

interfered in Turnatoria matters. But Commissar Popescu made a career of causing us grief. Failing to unseat me, he wired Mr. Fotiade to ask that all Jewish workers be replaced with Ukrainians. The request was denied.

At the end of our second winter in Moghilev, I decided that my resigning as committee president would improve our relations with Major Botoroaga, who was interested only in lining his pockets but could get nowhere with me. I chose as my successor Mr. Moses Katz, who had known the gendarme commander before the war. Major Botoroaga pretended to oppose my decision, so I insisted on a meeting with Colonel Loghin, to whom neither I nor any Jew had spoken since his arrival. The prefect received me and approved my resignation on the grounds that the Turnatoria kept me too busy with other Jewish problems.

Major Botoroaga demanded and received a great amount of protection money from the new committee but continued abusing Jews. I criticized Moses Katz privately for graft and dereliction of duty but stopped short of deposing him because of what Major Botoroaga might do in retaliation.

# 4

# VAPNIARCA

Having failed to free my four colleagues from Vapniarca, I wrote the following letter to Governor Alexianu on July 3, 1943:

". . . More than a month has passed since members of my committee . . . were sent to Vapniarca as a result of a denunciation by Mr. Tugui. . . .

"As president of the Jewish Committee and therefore responsible for all its decisions, my exemption gives the false impression that I sacrificed the others to save myself, which casts me in a bad light. The order to send those people to Vapniarca predated the verdict of the military court in Tiraspol, which exonerated the accused, finding that Mr. Tugui had demanded the gratuity by threatening to give you a negative report. As the matter now stands, I ask you, Mr. Governor, very respectfully, to reexamine this case and return these people to their families in Moghilev. I submit that these four men from the beginning have been faithful co–workers, laboring day and night to achieve the results we now show. I miss their contributions. Should you not be able to approve my request, then I ask politely and respectfully that you send me to Vapniarca in their place."

The four were released a month later. Upon his return to Moghilev, Dr. Jonas Kessler reported that about one-quarter of the prison population in Vapniarca had suffered paralysis after being fed a poisonous strain of peas. Prison officials dispensed no medicine to alleviate the acute pain of the victims.

On October 13, 1943, a delegate from Vapniarca brought me a letter signed by Mr. Paul Donath, informing me that in a few days the prison Lager would be moved to the district of Oceacov, a move that would doom those too sick to travel. The letter ended with an appeal for help: "We believe that you are not indifferent to our fate."

I pledged my support but found no solution. Then a miracle occurred. Moghilev's Mayor, Captain Nicolae Botta, paid me a visit after returning from a trip to Transylvania, where he met an old friend who had been offered the command of Vapniarca. Mr. Botta suggested that his friend, Colonel Sabin Motora, a man of exceptional character, apply instead to become prefect of Moghilev. I asked Mr. Botta to wire his friend immediately and convince him to accept the Vapniarca commission.

The next day Mr. Botta told me that Colonel Motora had agreed. I thanked the mayor and asked him to set up a meeting between Colonel Motora and me in the Turnatoria the following Saturday morning.

At the prescribed time, a car pulled into the factory compound and out stepped a handsome Romanian colonel, decorated with German medals. He asked to have his auto repaired and, according to plan, was told by the director of our auto shop that he would have to talk with Engineer Jagendorf in the Turnatoria head office. No one else knew the purpose of his visit.

I informed the colonel that transferring the prison camp to Oceacov would result in the deaths of hundreds of paralyzed prisoners. Living up to his good name, Colonel Motora agreed to oppose the relocation plan. Then I asked him if Mr. Paul Donath, the Jewish leader at Vapniarca, could meet me in Moghilev. "You know, Engineer Jagendorf," he said, "I cannot issue travel authorizations to political prisoners." Acknowledging the problem, I suggested a plan: "We cannot repair your car today, but if you sent it back tomorrow, we will do the job on Monday. Would you instruct Mr. Donath, under guard, to deliver the vehicle in the morning? I will need him for a few days, the time it takes to make the repairs." The colonel agreed to the plan.

The following morning at 10:00 A.M., Mr. Donath arrived at my office and asked me for an explanation. I revealed how Colonel Motora had become commander of Vapniarca. He looked at me in disbelief and said, "This must be a dream." We talked for a few hours, then wrote letters to Bucharest informing our underground contacts about the situation in the prison camp. The relocation order was cancelled and most of the Vapniarca inmates survived the war under the protection of Colonel Sabin Motora.

# 5

---

# FILDERMAN IN
# MOGHILEV

A SHOCKING event occurred on June 1, 1943. Dr. Wilhelm Filderman, the most influential Jew in all of Romania, the man to whom we looked for deliverance, arrived in Moghilev as a deportee. We took this to mean that all of us would go in the way prescribed by Hitler and Antonescu.

Dr. Filderman, an attorney and veteran Jewish leader, began his illustrious career when he represented us at Versailles following the first world war. He joined the United States representative, Louis Brandeis, in demanding that Romania grant full citizenship to Jews as a condition for territorial concessions. As a result, Romania acquired Bukovina and Bessarabia, and the Jews gained civil rights.

Dr. Filderman presided over the Union of the Jewish Communities in Romania until December, 1941, when the Antonescu regime outlawed the organization, which later was replaced by the Jewish Center. Undeterred by his dismissal, Dr. Filderman spoke out boldly against the anti-Semitic injustices of the military dictatorship. The Romanian government tolerated the veteran Jewish leader's intercessions, but his opposition to a forced Jewish contribution of four billion lei so infuriated Antonescu that the dictator personally banished Dr. Filderman to Transnistria.

Now the great Romanian Jewish leader and his wife were in Moghilev. I considered going to the gendarmerie to seek a meeting with Dr. Filderman but chose not to give Major Botoroaga the satisfaction of denying my request. Instead, I sent Dr. Jonas Kessler to inform Dr. Filderman, who was very ill, that Hilda and I were making arrangements for their care.

The next morning, Dr. Pokorny, a Romanian friend who managed a nearby sugar plant, came to see me in the Turnatoria. "Mr. Jagendorf," he said, "take good care of Dr. Filderman. They have plans for him."

"What do you mean?"

"I have just come from the gendarmerie, where I overheard Major Botoroaga asking a young doctor what the fastest way would be to send Filderman to heaven. The doctor said, 'Put him in the hospital and I'll see to the rest.' Botoroaga said that he had strict orders to place Filderman in the ghetto. They left the matter unresolved."

I found the Fildermans a room across the road from my house. When we met, I advised them to eat all their meals with us and to avoid accepting food or drink from anyone else. We assigned our best doctors to Dr. Filderman and posted a Jewish sentry at his door around the clock.

A few days later, a German officer handed me a copy of a Berlin newspaper carrying an editorial titled: *"Der Jude Filderman"* (The Jew Filderman), applauding the deportation of the man who made "Jewish politics" in Romania. The Nazis made no secret of their desire to have the outspoken Jewish leader silenced permanently.

Late one evening, while escorting the Fildermans home after a meeting in our apartment, we spotted a German patrol leaving their room. The intruders approached us and asked me, "Are you Filderman?"

"No," I replied.

"Who are you then, and what are you doing on the street at this hour?"

"I am Engineer Siegfried Jagendorf, director of the Turnatoria. I have the authority to be anywhere in Moghilev at any time. At the moment, I am on my way to inspect the night shift, if you will excuse us." We walked away.

The next day I called on the German commander to protest the incident. He promised that nothing like that would happen again, and nothing did. When we reached the Turnatoria, Dr. Filderman told me that General Constantin Vasiliu, the national chief of police, had assured him that his stay in Moghilev would last no more than three months.

Dr. Filderman worked diligently, analyzing our instructions and receiving visitors. He advised the committee on all matters, from finance to education, promising to intensify his efforts to help us after his return to Romania, a promise he would keep.

# 6

## BEYOND THE BUG

I N MID-OCTOBER, 1943, I learned that a Jew who had recently arrived in Moghilev from a Lager beyond the Bug sought a meeting with me. He was accompanied by a German officer. I instructed Dr. Kessler to run a check on the Jew. He promptly reported that Nathan Segall of Cernauti had an excellent reputation and could be trusted. I invited Mr. Segall to the Turnatoria and listened to his story:

"On August 18, 1942, at 6:30 A.M., the Lager Ladijin in the district of Tulcin was surrounded by SS troops and Lithuanian militia under the command of SS Obersturmführer Christoffel and SS Oberscharführer Maass. Our group, which I headed, numbered 400 souls.

"In the morning, they began an arbitrary selection of the deportees, without regard to the age or physical condition. I, my wife, and two daughters were chosen to remain, while my widowed sister-in-law and her two sons had to leave. I chose to evacuate our entire family.

"We had precisely thirty minutes to pack. As we climbed into waiting trucks, the guards set upon us with their whips. At the shore of the Bug River, articles of value were confiscated. Women and children crossed over a bridge; the men had to swim. Fortunately, none of us drowned. On the other side, German police demanded our money. Afterwards, we were divided into smaller groups and dispersed by truck to Mihailovca, Crasnopolca, Terasivca, and Ivangorod.

"Our group was brought to a fifty-yard-long horse stable in Mihailovca, occupied by some several hundred Ukrainian Jews who no longer looked human. I asked Sergeant Kiesel of the German police to segregate us from these Jews because we still had clean clothes. He permitted us to camp in a courtyard enclosed by barbed wire. The following morning at 6:00 A.M., we were assigned highway work. The German Lager commander appointed me as the chief Jew. In this position I had the opportunity to make contact with a few Germans who belonged to Organization Todt. Among them I found understanding and warmth. We slept outside until a second stable became available, which would serve as our home for the next three months.

"On the second or third day, our group was assigned to a soldier who could dispose of us as he pleased. He greeted us by shooting two old men, M. Seodner and C. Zuker. Later, mathematics professor M. Kirmayer and several others suffered the same fate.

"On the second Sunday of our stay, SS men appeared at 8:30 A.M. and ordered all Jews to stand in the yard with our luggage and declare their valuables. Fearing for their lives, most of the people handed over everything they had—shoes, furs, clothes, soap—and watched helplessly as their last earthly possessions were carted away.

"The Lithuanian guards routinely shot ten to fifteen Jewish workers each week. A human life had no value to those primitive peasants. They would shoot a Jew for his boots or a gold-filled tooth. One rarely saw a clothed corpse.

"Every word voiced by the Lithuanians was a curse or threat: 'Remember, Jew, if you tell anybody what's happening here, your life is finished.'

"One morning after the fourth week, sixty people were lined up and shot. Similar actions claimed more than a hundred lives on one occasion, fifty on another.

"On the night of November 3, 1942, we awoke under a blanket of snow. Some of our people had typhus, but I concealed this information from the SS to forestall further shootings. The massacres stopped between November and March, 1943, but resumed with the arrival of SS Oberscharführer Maass, who ordered the victims to dig their own graves."

After finishing his story, Mr. Segall asked me for help. Since he would pass through Tulcin on his return trip, I told Mr. Segall to see Prefect Nasturas and tell him exactly what awaited Jews sent beyond the Bug River. He did so, and the prefect offered him sanctuary, but Mr. Segall refused, choosing to return to his wife and two daughters who had remained in the German Lager.

Colonel Nasturas told me that he had no authority to request the return of Jews from the German side of the Bug without written orders from Bucharest, either authentic or counterfeit. I wrote Dr. Filderman, urgently requesting the necessary papers, but none came.

# 7

---

# ODESSA

THE GOVERNMENT decided to exploit a large peat bog in the Tulcin district for the manufacture of heating briquettes. Engineer Popescu and I were called to Odessa by Mr. Fotiade to discuss plans for fabricating the necessary dehydrating apparatus. After receiving a cordial welcome, I presented a production plan and projected delivery dates. Engineer Popescu disputed the schedule, insisting that the Turnatoria could meet an earlier deadline. At that point, I derided the commissar for his ignorance about the matter under discussion and his general ineptitude as a factory manager. Mr. Fotiade approved my projected deadlines.

While in Odessa, I visited Colonel Mihail P. Iliescu, the chief gendarme inspector, to renew our acquaintanceship. I also used the occasion to pick up medical supplies requested by the Turnatoria pharmacist. Although permitted full access to this beautiful port city on the Black Sea, I chose to remain with a handful of Jewish artisans who worked in a small ghetto. Before the invasion, Odessa had been a flourishing Jewish center, the largest in the Soviet Union.

Immediately upon my return, we began drafting blueprints for briquette ovens. I used the opportunity to add 300 young apprentices to the Turnatoria's work force. Unfortunately, we also received an order to send Jewish work brigades to the peat bogs of Tulcin. Only with great effort did we recover these people, who returned half dead from having to dig peat by hand while standing in the frigid marshes.

The war was going badly for the Germans. One could feel the tension among the military officials in Moghilev. The large order from the peat plant in Tulcin suddenly was cancelled. The authorities in Odessa directed us to begin dismantling certain factories and shops in Moghilev in preparation for transporting machines to Romania. Antonescu was terminating our life-support system. I wrote to Dr. Filderman, recommending that our specialists be transferred to Romania, but nothing came of it.

On December 20, 1943, the deported Jews from Dorohoi received their repatriation orders, raising our hopes that we might soon follow. We feared, however, that the retreating Germans would liquidate us first.

# Spring–Summer, 1943

GERMANY AND her Axis partners lost ground throughout 1943. In March, U.S. and Australian bombers destroyed a key Japanese convoy in the Bismarck Sea. In May, Axis forces surrendered in Tunisia. In July, United States and British forces landed in Sicily, and Allied aircraft bombed Rome. In August, the Soviets recaptured Orel and Kharkov.

Deportations of Jews to death camps continued from distant points throughout Europe. In March, the Greek Jews of Macedonia and Thrace (both occupied by Bulgaria) were deported to Treblinka. Two weeks later, more than 43,000 Jews from Salonika, Greece, boarded trains to Auschwitz–Birkenau, while Dutch and French Jews departed for Sobibor. Then, thousands of Jews from Cracow were liquidated. The nearly 50,000 Jews of Bulgaria, a German ally, were saved when King Boris III, the Parliament, and the citizenry united in opposing their deportation to Nazi extermination camps.

In the first civilian uprising against German occupation forces anywhere in Europe, the Jewish Fighters Organization of the Warsaw ghetto staged an armed revolt on April 19, 1943, that caught the Nazis unprepared. After suffering initial setbacks, the Germans resorted to incinerating the Jewish quarter block by block. It was not until May 16, 1943, after a conflagration of almost four weeks, that General Juergen Stroop could finally report to Berlin, "the Warsaw ghetto exists no more."

In May and June, 1943, additional thousands of Jews arrived in Auschwitz–Birkenau from Holland, Croatia, Salonika, Belgium, and France. In eastern Galicia, German killing units wiped out one Jewish community after another. SS Reichsführer Heinrich Himmler ordered the final liquidation of the Polish ghettos on June 11, 1943.

---

In Romania, the Jews were subjected to ever-increasing financial burdens in the form of real estate and business confiscations, punitive taxes, mandatory "loans" or "contributions," and payments in lieu of forced labor. In May, 1943, Marshal Antonescu ordered the Jewish community to raise a contribution of four billion lei (twenty million dollars). Dr. Wilhelm Filderman told Dr. Nandor Gingold, head of the Jewish Center that he would resist the unrealistic demand. Gingold informed the Romanian authorities of Filderman's opposition, prompting the enraged director to banish the irrepressible Jewish leader to Transnistria.

Rabbi Alexandre Safran recounts in his memoir, *Resisting the Storm*, his attempt to keep Dr. Filderman in Bucharest:

"I immediately initiated my own interventions in order to obtain the cancellation of the Marshal's order. Employing the testimony of Doctors Teodorescu and Lupu, I sought to demonstrate that Filderman was a sick man. They suggested that Filderman enter the Victoria Sanatorium, and he was indeed admitted. There, the doctor purposely caused Filderman's fever to rise in order to substantiate the illness concocted by me in order to avoid his deportation."

Dr. Filderman's fever did not affect the order. He and his wife, who went voluntarily, were put on a train that arrived in Moghilev on June 1, 1943. The Nazis would have preferred to have the influential Jew killed, but Antonescu wanted only to teach him a lesson. In Moghilev, Major Botoroaga reportedly conspired with Dr. Ionescu to assassinate Filderman, but they took no action. A document in the Filderman Archive at Yad Vashem refers to the second incident: "One night in July, 1943, three men from Organization Todt entered Filderman's home, but at the time he was with neighbors, the Jagendorfs, so he escaped." The report adds, "Two days before he (Filderman) left Moghilev, someone shot through his window, but nobody was hurt."

Initially, the deportees in Moghilev regarded Filderman's deportation with foreboding, but his hands-on involvement in the affairs of the colony and accessibility calmed the people, and his repatriation to Romania at the end of August, 1943, rekindled their hope. It should be noted that although Filderman had been stripped of office and the right to practice law, he was regarded by the Romanian government as the foremost Jewish leader. The ultimate success of Filderman's diplomacy amid such virulent anti-Semitism rested on his personal stature as a veteran communal leader and anti-Communist, and on his tactic of formulating his interventions in patriotic terms. Filderman repeatedly professed his people's past and present loyalty to the Romanian cause and argued that the mistreatment and massacre of Jews was inimical to the national interest.

Filderman fled Communist Romania in 1948 to escape arrest on charges of spying for Great Britain. He lived his remaining years in Paris, maintaining contact with Jagendorf and other Romanian Jewish figures.

He died in 1963 at age 81, before completing his autobiography.

---

By May, 1943, the second typhus epidemic in Moghilev had been brought under control and not a single death was reported in the three orphanages. Having achieved these goals, Jagendorf installed Moses Katz, an engineer, as head of the Jewish Committee, by this time synonymous with the district labor office. Katz refused to be dominated by his predecessor, resulting in a bitter power struggle over who would control the distribution of aid in the district. Katz argued that this function belonged to the labor office, whereas Jagendorf insisted that the Jewish Center had specifically entrusted the job to him. In retaliation, Katz complained to the authorities that Jagendorf had padded the Turnatoria work force; Jagendorf hit back by trying to seize control of the cooperative trade shops. In September, 1943, a Jagendorf supporter, signing "Dorel," wrote to Dr. Filderman, calling for the dismissal of Moses Katz. He recommended that all assistance from Bucharest be administered by Siegfried Jagendorf who, "as you know, is ambitious and honor-chasing, but also has three virtues: exactness, objectivity, and energy—all indispensable in these troubled times."

---

Jagendorf waged a long and acrimonious struggle against the government watchdog inside the Turnatoria, Engineer Eugen Popescu, a Romanian who conspired to unseat Jagendorf and replace the Jewish work force with Ukrainian Christians. On March 26, 1943, Jagendorf informed Prefect Nasturas that Popescu had done nothing to stop Ukrainian workers from committing acts of sabotage and theft. The next day, Jagendorf followed up with a confidential report, accusing Popescu of stealing fuel, bypassing the labor office in hiring unqualified Ukrainians, and hazardously storing a large quantity of kerosene. On July 25, 1943, Jagendorf wrote to the director of industry, Ion Fotiade:

"Despite your order, he (Popescu) has not changed his behavior, insulting me all the time. He said to me, 'You are a nobody. You are the Jew Jagendorf, and I am the government. I can send you any time to a Lager. I will order the gendarmes to arrest you for sabotage. When I enter your office, you have to stand up. I will throw you out of your office.' This happened today in front of seven workers. This is why I tell you that Popescu and I cannot coexist. His attitude is destroying this factory, for which I have sacrificed my health. I therefore request that you request my resignation as director of the factory."

Fotiade refused to ask for Jagendorf's resignation; he also declined to dismiss Popescu, whose influential friends could have had Fotiade court-martialed for choosing a Jew over a Christian. During this contest for control of the factory, Moghilev received its third prefect, Colonel Constantin Loghin, who as his first public act, announced the firing of Jagendorf. The prefect's display of bravado backfired. Jagendorf's reorganization scheme had shifted administrative control of the Turnatoria from the district prefecture to the provincial government in Odessa. Had Jagendorf failed to take this defensive measure, Loghin and Botoroaga might easily have gained the upper hand, dismissing Jagendorf as Turnatoria director and eliminating the Jewish workers who had rebuilt the city's state-run enterprises.

After the war, Jagendorf had the last word in his feud with Eugen Popescu. In an affidavit submitted to the People's Court, he testified that the former government commissar had tortured Jewish and Ukrainian workers, stolen 500,000 lei ($2,500) from Natan Klipper while acting as a courier between Bucharest and Moghilev, looted the Turnatoria warehouse following the retreat of the Romanian Army, and engaged in blackmail.

---

The Romanian authorities complained constantly that Jagendorf had packed the Turnatoria with a redundancy of Jews. On July 13, 1943, for example, Major Botoroaga, Moghilev's third gendarme commander, wrote a sharp note to the engineer: "I asked you not to hire anymore Turnatoria workers. This is a camouflage and I don't like it." Three days later, Jagendorf replied that only a small number of applicants actually were hired, justifying a small increase in personnel by documenting an increase in factory productivity. Jagendorf added, "I ask you to punish those informers who are giving you false information. . . . You now have the facts, but I ask you to send a commission of inquiry to find out the truth, and to punish those who try to slander the committee." Had the commander called Jagendorf's bluff, he might have discovered that in the lathe department, for instance, of 130 workers, only ten were skilled and the remainder trainees, some as young as thirteen.

Major Botoroaga preferred to prey on the more vulnerable non-Turnatoria Jews in Moghilev, pressing them into forced labor battalions for service in mines, forests, marshes, and other perilous sites. On the first day of May, 1943, for example, 1,555 Jews from the Moghilev ghetto were selected to aid the Germans in constructing a bridge over the Bug River. Prefect Loghin requested specifically that the battalion include the ghetto's intelligentsia. The Jews labored 14–15 hours a day, sustained by one bowl of soup and 200 grams of bread. The Germans disqualified 500 men as unfit and proposed that they be returned to Moghilev. Major Botoroaga refused to take them back, but reconsidered upon receiving a gem worth 500,000 lei ($2,500). The "unfit" workers never reached Moghilev; the gendarme commander rerouted them to Trihati, a Lager in the southeastern corner of Transnistria, far from their families.

Major Gheorghe Botoroaga was convicted as a war criminal in July, 1945, and sentenced to hard labor for life, loss of civil rights for ten years, and confiscation of property. His predecessor, Major Romeo Orasanu received twenty years at hard labor, and loss of civil rights and property. Both were released in 1955, when the Communist government of Romania pardoned or reduced the sentences of imprisoned war criminals.

Alexandre Safran, who in 1940 at the age of thirty became chief rabbi of Romania, was forced to leave his country in December, 1947, for refusing to cooperate with the Jewish Communists who were engaged in a power struggle against Dr. Filderman and the traditional Jewish leadership. Rabbi Safran settled in Geneva, Switzerland, where he serves as chief rabbi.

# Part Seven

# 1944–1946

SYNAGOGUE

*Jagendorf Archives, Yad Vashem, The Holocaust Martyrs' and Heroes' Remembrance Authority, Jerusalem*

# 1

# FAREWELL MOGHILEV

O<small>N</small> M<small>ARCH</small> 2, 1944, Major Botoroaga handed me a wire from Bucharest ordering me and Hilda to return to Radauti. The major told us to begin making preparations and to inform him when we were ready. Major Botoroaga had the power to forcibly evacuate us; in fact, it was his duty to do so. The repatriation action had been initiated and arranged by Dr. Filderman.

I returned to my offices and met with Dr. Hillel Brender, Dr. Jonas Kessler, and David Rennert. They regarded the news as a miracle, in view of the growing threat of the retreating Nazi troops heading our way.

"We've had enough trouble with the few Germans already here," one said. "Imagine what will happen to us when their retreating forces sweep through the city. Leave and take up our cause in Bucharest. Perhaps you will have more success there." They all agreed.

Several days passed and I still had not decided on a departure date. Finally Major Botoroaga summoned me and said, "You must leave tomorrow morning. The escort will meet you and your family at 6:00 A.M."

I went home and started packing my belongings. Hundreds

LEGIUNEA DE JANDARMI MOGHILEV

Nr.    din 7.III.1944.

ACT DE LEGITIMATIE SI CALATORIE Nr.

In conformitate cu dispoziţiunile Preşedenţiei
Cosniliului de Miniştri:

    Evreul Ing. Iägendorf Siegfried cap de familie înso-
ţit de  membrii de familie menţionaţi pe verso,
călătoreşte din Transnistria dela Moghilev în
orasul Rădăuţi, unde i s'a stabilit domiciliul.-

    La sosirea în orasul Rădăuţi capul de familie
se va prezenta în termen de 24 ore poliţiei
respective, unde va depune prezentul act de
legitımaţie, pe baza căruia  se va elibera
buletin de înscriere la biroul populaţiei pentru
toţi membrii familiei conform legii.-

    Pleacă astăzi 7 Martie, anul 1944.
    Comandantul Legiunei Jand.Moghilev
    ss. Indescifrabil
    (L.S.).

conformitate

*Jagendorf's authorization to travel with his family from Moghilev to Radauti.
Issued by the Legion of Gendarmes, the document states, "He's leaving today,
March 7, 1944."*

of people had gathered in the yard to say goodbye. Mr. Fred
Saraga, the representative of the Jewish Center, who was in
Moghilev at the time, paid our train fare.

    In the morning, we walked silently to the railway station,
accompanied by a large crowd. I felt great sadness and guilt
about leaving all these people. As the train pulled out of the
station and headed towards the new bridge, the well-wishers
waved. Looking at them, I thought about our arrival here,

and all we had gone through together. And now I was taking leave of them, just as the hardest blow of all was about to strike—the German army! Paula Scharf wrote a farewell poem:

*More than two years have passed*
*Since the dark powers of fate*
*Severed us from the family of man.*
*And our houses empty remained.*

*Gloomy despair and bitter distress*
*Were our companions then.*
*We stood before the Dniester paralyzed.*
*And our stomachs empty remained.*

*Then you came, a man of courage,*
*You gave us a foundry, a sanctuary.*
*Set us free of misfortune and sorrow,*
*And our pride you restored.*

*We stood firm, unbroken*
*Human beings once again.*
*They banished and beat us*
*But our honor you defended.*

*Now you take leave of us.*
*Those bound to you*
*By the torment and the triumph.*
*But our hopes with you tarry.*

*Forget not that death approaches.*
*We are forsaken, lost.*
*Break not the faith you swore,*
*And come for us soon.*

Did they regard me as a traitor? They must have known that my decision to leave was in their best interest, that I would never forsake them to save my own skin. The train moved slowly over the river, the water peaceful now.

# 2

# BUKOVINA, BOTOSANI, BUCHAREST

After twenty-four hours, we arrived in Cernauti. Our two gendarme escorts permitted us a two-day respite in this city of our former life. They guarded our belongings as Mrs. Jagendorf and I struggled up the steep hill from the railway station into the city. My sick wife, who stayed in bed much of the time in Moghilev, could hardly walk. At last we arrived at the house of a dear friend. He embraced us with body and heart. At last we could sleep in a real bed and eat a good meal. News of our presence in Cernauti spread fast. People came day and night to ask about their loved ones in Transnistria.

At the agreed upon time, we rejoined our escorts at the train station for the last forty miles of our journey to Radauti. In anticipation of our arrival, the town's few remaining Jews, knowing we had no money, prepared a fully stocked room for us and extended their hospitality to our escorts as well. In the morning, we were handed over to the Radauti police chief, who received us kindly.

Radauti, my wife's native town, had a population of approximately 25,000 people. As a young engineer working for Siemens–Schukert, I had worked on the town's first power plant. Radauti had an international reputation for its famous performing horses bred by Mr. Ion Larionescu, my non-Jewish friend who had helped us by ordering stoves from the Turnatoria and later was jailed for aiding other Jews in Transnistria.

Soon after our arrival, people began evacuating, a sign that the Red Army had broken through German lines. At the advice of friends, we "disappeared" to the country and found shelter in the home of a peasant. We returned to Radauti after learning that the Russians had occupied the city.

A Soviet officer asked me to recommend a candidate for prefect of Radauti. I submitted the name of Ion Larionescu, who had been released from prison. Mr. Larionescu became the new prefect and invited me to serve as his adviser. Hilda and I moved into the prefectura.

A few days later, a delegation of Russian partisans arrived in the city and, after thanking me for my assistance in Moghilev, reported that ten days after my departure the Germans made a headlong retreat through Moghilev and over the Dniester, blasting the bridge even before all their units had crossed. The Jews, they said, took care of the stray Germans and captured entire trainloads of food and other supplies. Much to my relief and joy, they reported that all Jews in Moghilev had been liberated. This turned out to be untrue. The Russians had detained many of the Turnatoria workers as well as other deportees.

The German Army retreated to a line twelve miles south of Radauti. Several weeks later, before the Soviets renewed their offensive, the town's entire population was evacuated to Siret, about ten miles north of Radauti. Upon our return, the Russian commander recommended that I take a top position in the prefectura. I had never belonged to a political party and did not want to start now. Hilda was ill and tired. Our only desire was to get a room with a good bed and bath, to convalesce after those long brutal years. Our needs meant nothing to the Soviets, who ordered me to recondition the town's power and water plants.

After completing the job, I wrote to Dr. Goldhammer, an old friend in the industrial city of Botosani, about forty miles southeast of Radauti, and asked for help in finding a room with a bath. When I arrived, Dr. Goldhammer escorted me to a fifteen-room estate surrounded by flower gardens. "The property is at your disposal," he said. "It belonged to a Romanian landowner and banker who has fled to Bucharest." A few days later, Hilda and I took up residence in the splendid house.

We discovered that a group of orphaned children from Moghilev had been placed in Botosani. The children greeted us with great excitement. We also met survivors of the Vapniarca Lager. They told us how Colonel Motora had resisted a German plan to execute all the inmates. I met old friends and started to relax.

After a few days, Dr. Goldhammer and the prefect appeared at the door. When I asked to what I owed the honor of their visit, they invited me to become mayor.

"I am an engineer, not an administrator," I replied, declining the offer. But no argument could convince the prefect that I was not up to the task. The Russian commander endorsed the prefect's effort to draft me into public service, and the next day I was sworn in as Botosani's first Jewish mayor.

I soon discovered that the area's only power plant was being dismantled for shipment to the Soviet Union. I rushed from one Russian authority to another, explaining that we had no alternate source of electricity. They ignored my protestations. Finally I persuaded the Russian engineer in charge of the operation to relinquish several key components from which we could reconstruct the system.

I traveled to Bucharest to offer my assistance to Dr. Filderman, who was laboring on behalf of the repatriated Jews, and used the opportunity to find an apartment in the capital. In October, 1944, I resigned as Mayor of Botosani and moved to Bucharest. Our rent-free apartment at Putual de Piatra 4 housed the mayor and a high-ranking Russian general. We had to borrow money from friends to cover moving costs and Mrs. Jagendorf's medical bills. I turned down all job offers, fearing that employment might delay our emigration. We contacted our children in America and asked them to send money and arrange for visas.

Letters from former deportees arrived by the sack. We received bad news from Moghilev. Many Turnatoria workers had been drafted into the Red Army. Their families sought my intervention. Deportees returning to Romania filed for repossession of their houses and properties, confiscated under the "Romanization" laws. My interventions with various high-level Russian officers concerning the return of Jewish properties to their rightful owners failed. It was not Jewish but Romanian property, they insisted, ignoring my explanation as to how the real estate had changed hands.

The Joint Distribution Committee, under the leadership of Dr. Filderman, did an excellent job of aiding the returnees. I concentrated my efforts on securing the release of Jews trapped in Transnistria and in the Cernauti area, which Stalin reclaimed as Soviet territory. The Red Army established strict border controls, permitting no person to cross into Romania without proper authorization from Moscow. The enslavement of the Jewish exiles in Transnistria would continue even after the fall of the Third Reich.

# 3

## THE PEOPLE'S COURT

ALL ROMANIAN officials who had served in Transnistria were suspected of war crimes by the People's Court. Several of them asked me for letters attesting to their humanitarian efforts on behalf of the exiles. I supplied the court with depositions, basing my testimony on the archives of the Jewish Committee, which I had brought out of Moghilev at the time of my departure. Many of the criminals, including Constantin Loghin, Gheorghe Botoroaga, and Romeo Orasanu, were sentenced to prison terms of twenty years to life. The trials exposed the atrocities committed in the various districts of Transnistria. The Romanian newspaper *Lupta Moldovei*, for example, reported on May 24, 1945, that in the district of Golta, Prefect Modest Isopescu plundered 70,000 innocent Jews before having them shot and their bodies cremated en masse.

Our good friend in the prefectura of Moghilev, Mr. Gheorghe Fuciu, was arrested in Brasov, Transylvania. He had in his possession a letter expressing my appreciation for everything he had done on our behalf. The investigating committee sent the letter to the Bucharest police for authentication. At the police station, after affirming that I had signed the letter, I made the following declaration:

". . . I met Mr. Fuciu soon after our arrival in Moghilev. Since all the industries were administered by Mr. Fuciu, he was influential in keeping Jews in Moghilev. As a matter of fact, this action was responsible for saving ten thousand Jews who otherwise would have been driven over the Bug River and killed. Mr. Fuciu was one of the few who in that time of persecution showed himself to be a human being in the true sense of the word, helping us whenever he could without any material interest and often against orders from his superiors. As a result, he had been investigated by the government of Transnistria. Mr. Fuciu assisted in the rescue of a great number of Jews, including more than 1,500 orphan children. . . ."

After the investigating committee received my declaration, Mr. Fuciu not only was released but commended and offered a government position.

During that period, Major Dr. Chirila asked me to visit him at his Bucharest office. He had been reinstated as general director of hospitals, but questions had been raised about his wartime activities in Transnistria. When I arrived, Dr. Chirila introduced me to a panel of people, then left the room. I answered all their inquiries, after which they called in Dr. Chirila and announced that henceforth he would have no more difficulties.

About that time, Mr. Fotiade's brother came to see me. The former Transnistria official wanted me to visit him in the prefectura jail. I promised to see him the next day. When I arrived, Mr. Fotiade said, "I do not know how you feel about my behavior toward you and the other Jews in Moghilev. I did nothing against you. I tried to have Engineer Popescu removed, but he had powerful people behind him. If you believe that my behavior was correct, please put it in writing so that I can get out of here."

I told him that I would have to refer to my documents and promised to return the following day. At home, I wrote a letter thanking him for opposing Colonel Loghin's move to fire me, rejecting Engineer Popescu's proposal to replace Jewish workers with Ukrainians, and helping us acquire food. The next day I personally delivered the letter. As he read it, tears filled his eyes. Unable to speak, he pressed my hand. Maybe my letter convinced this former Iron Guard leader that he had been wrong about us.

The following day I was summoned before the People's Court, where the prosecutor asked me to authenticate my letter to Fotiade. He then asked me if I knew anything about the accused's activities in Odessa. I said no. Mr. Fotiade soon was released.

Mr. Paul Donath, the former Jewish leader in Vapniarca, asked me to help him reorganize the electrical industries of Romania. I declined, even though we were in dire need of money, explaining that I soon would be leaving the country and didn't want to take on responsibilities that might complicate matters. At about the same time, the organization of the Romanian industrialists needed to import machinery from Austria and Czechoslovakia, but every qualified purchasing agent they proposed to send abroad was denied an exist visa by the Soviet authorities. A friend of mine in the organization, convinced that I would have no difficulty with the ministry, offered me an attractive commission, which I decided to accept.

While waiting for the visa, Mrs. Filderman notified me that her husband had been interrogated by the Russians. They suspected him of subversive activities. I felt obliged to investigate the matter and learned that Dr. Filderman had been placed under house arrest. I asked Hilda to pay a social call to Mrs. Filderman. At the Fildermans' apartment, my wife was met by a sentry who asked her to identify herself and state her business. As she was doing so, both Dr. and Mrs. Filderman came to the door and, assuring her that they were alright, advised Hilda to go home.

The next morning two Romanian security men came to our apartment and asked me to accompany them to the station for the purpose of identifying a prisoner named "Berger," who claimed to know me. They asked me to bring along my passport for identification purposes. I told them that the passport was at the ministry with my visa application. We drove for more than half an hour before reaching a heavily fortified building. Inside, I was led to a room and told to wait. A man soon entered and asked me to give a detailed report of how Romanian officials had behaved in Transnistria. I invited him to come to my apartment, where I kept the relevant documentation. He replied, "I am a very busy man and cannot spare the time. I will need only a very short description."

"All right, I shall try to prepare it for you," I said.

"When could I get it?"

"By Saturday."

"Fine. I shall call you then, and we will arrange to meet in the city."

"But I thought you wanted to talk with me about Mr. Berger."

"Yes. We will talk about him on Saturday."

The episode troubled me. I asked my escort where we were. "You are in the Malmison prison," he said, ordering the guards to escort me out.

I wrote up my report and waited for the prosecutor's call. It never came. On Sunday I learned through my contacts that the Romanian secret service had confiscated my passport, suspecting that I might try to enlist foreign support on behalf of Dr. Filderman.

After six months, a government agent came to our apartment and informed me that the investigation had been concluded and I was free to leave the country. On May 20, 1946, Hilda and I received a one-way passport out of Romania. Our citizenship had been revoked.

I desperately wanted to get out, but securing a foreign visa proved difficult. The American consulate had not opened, and the French consulate had rejected my application. I succeeded finally in obtaining a thirty-day transit visa through Prague, Czechoslovakia.

We boarded the train early but found two Russian officers sitting in our compartment. They refused to vacate, ignoring the conductor's insistence that the seats were ours. We had to stand on the platform with our luggage. At the last minute, the Russian railroad police evicted the stubborn officers. So went our last experience in Romania.

# 4

## TO AMERICA

$W$E ARRIVED at the Prague train station in mid-October, 1946, and were met by friends who had been with us in Transnistria. They provided us with all kinds of foods, courtesy of the United Nations. Seven weeks later, the U.S. consulate in Prague issued us visas, and I booked a flight to New York via Copenhagen. But first we needed to secure a transit visa through Denmark. The Danish consulate in Prague advised me to write directly to Copenhagen. After two weeks without a reply, I wired a friend in Copenhagen for help; a few days later the visa arrived. By that time, our Prague transit visa had expired, and my application for an extension was denied. They told us to return to Romania. We chose instead to go underground until the departure day.

We landed at La Guardia Field on December 23, 1946. As we taxied to the terminal, I saw from the portal our daughter, Elfreda, her husband, and their three-year-old son, Ralph. I pointed them out to Hilda, who couldn't believe it was true. Nobody thought she would survive, but her intense desire to be reunited with our children and grandchildren fortified her will. Now she broke down. When our daughter Edith phoned from Dayton, Ohio, Hilda could not utter a sound. It took several calls before she was able to express in words her feelings at that miraculous moment.

At the immigration desk, a man in uniform looked at me and asked, "Did you help people in a concentration camp?" Startled by the question, I said, "If you know that I was in a concentration camp, then you also must know what I did there."

"I am well aware of your activities there," he replied. "Welcome to the United States."

*Commentary for Part Seven*

---

# 1944–1946

DURING THE fifth and final year of the war, the Soviets broke the siege of Leningrad and pushed the German forces across the Dnieper, Bug, Dniester, and Prut Rivers, capturing all of Bukovina and Odessa in April. That month, U.S. and British warplanes bombed Romania's Ploesti oil fields. On the western front, the Anglo–American invasion of Normandy began on June 6, 1944. Marshal Antonescu was arrested by King Michael on August 23, 1944. The next day, Romania signed an armistice with the Allies and declared war on Germany. A week later, the Red Army entered Bucharest. The Soviets took Warsaw, Cracow, and Lodz in January, 1945, Budapest in February, Danzig in March, and Vienna in April. Adolf Hitler committed suicide in his Berlin bunker on April 30, 1945. Germany surrendered a week later.

In the campaign against Europe's Jews, transports converged on Auschwitz–Birkenau at a furious pace. In March, 1944, the Hungarian government condemned a half-million Jews to death by permitting their deportation to that massive extermination center. In June, 1944, transports arrived from France, Italy, Holland, Corfu, and eastern Galicia. In August and September of the same year, the remaining 70,000 of the Lodz ghetto perished at Auschwitz, as did approximately 3,000 Jews from Holland and 4,000 from Theresienstadt. The Germans deported 8,000 Slovakian Jews to Auschwitz in October, 1944, one month before Heinrich Himmler finally ordered the gassings stopped. Two months later, on January 27, 1945, the Red Army liberated the darkest star in the Nazi constellation of some two thousand concentration and forced-labor camps throughout Europe. An estimated 1.5 million Jews (one-quarter of the total murdered in the Holocaust) perished at Auschwitz-Birkenau.

---

As the winter of 1943 approached, Ion Antonescu became increasingly concerned about his culpability in the tragedy of Transnistria. On November 17, 1943, the military dictator told his advisers that he would not tolerate the killing of approximately 50,000 surviving deportees in Transnistria by the retreating Germans because "these terrible murders" would give him "a bad reputation." The Marshal proposed returning the exiles to Romania but no action was taken until December 20, 1943, when 1,500 of the Dorohoi deportees received their repatriation orders. On March 6, 1944, two trains carrying 1,909 orphans arrived in Iasi, Romania from Transnistria—1,425 children from Moghilev and 484 children from the southern part of Transnistria.

———————

Dr. Wilhelm Filderman won approval for the Jagendorf's repatriation in December, 1943. In a letter dated January 27, 1944, Jagendorf thanked "Mr. Visan"—a code name for Dr. Filderman:

"Yesterday, F. (Fred Saraga) brought me your greetings and informed me that my repatriation has been settled. This fact, and also your gesture of support has pleased me tremendously. Please accept my heartfelt gratitude.

"I shall leave this place of worries and suffering with mixed feelings, despite the adversity, the work, and the concerns of the past thirty months. I feel as one with the suffering mass, forming its backbone, if I may say so.

"Knowing that I shall continue to work and care for the needy there, after having provided for my wife, will make the departure easier. For that reason, I ask you to intervene so that I might be able to come to Bucharest. My wife, as you well know, is very sick and urgently needs medical attention. . . .

"You were kind enough to let me know through Fred that the following persons should forward to you their applications: Isidor Pressner, Dr. Jonas Kessler, David Rennert, Dr. Gedalia Preminger, and Dr. Hillel Brender. F. will bring you the respective applications with all the necessary personal data. . . .

"I want to take this opportunity to thank you from the bottom of my heart, in the name of all the thousands of sufferers in Transnistria, for your exemplary, untiring, and sacrificial work. . . ."

Dr. Jonas Kessler, Jagendorf's faithful political adviser, chose to remain in Moghilev, explaining his reason in a letter to Dr. Filderman, dated January 30, 1944:

". . . More than ever, it is my duty to remain among those with whom I have suffered . . . hour by hour, minute by minute. They need me especially now that the engineer—against his will—is leaving us. . . .

"I want to and must stay at my post. I am needed not only by the 700 workers of the Turnatoria—with their families, almost 3,000 souls—but also by the ghetto. More than anybody, you, beloved maestro, will comprehend the necessity of my gesture. . . .

"I belong . . . to a postwar (World War I) generation, which has never had a day of joy—chicanery at high school, humiliation at university, exclusion from the profession, and deportation to death between the Dniester and Bug. And all that for an absurd, nonexistent guilt: to have been a Jew. . . .

"I and the others believe that your superhuman efforts for our just cause soon will free us from death's embrace. . . . I want to stay here as your humble collaborator and co-worker. Should your endeavors fail and we must share the fate of our unfortunate brothers over the Bug . . . we will die with these words on our lips: 'There are still men in Bucharest.' "

Dr. Filderman worked diligently to hasten the Jagendorfs' release. On February 11, 1944, he wrote to Mihai Antonescu (the second most powerful man in the government of Romania), asking him to expedite their homecoming. Filderman also contacted the national police minister, General Constantin Vasiliu, inquiring why repatriation orders had not been issued for the Jagendorfs, Moses Katz, and the sisters of the chief rabbi. While waiting for his papers, Jagendorf continued his rescue work in Transnistria. He wrote the following letter to Dr. Filderman on February 21, 1944:

". . . I must again bring up the cause of the Jews in Tulcin. . . . After the visit of Mr. Nathan Segall, I wrote to you requesting urgently that you arrange to have an order sent to the prefect of Tulcin [Nasturas], asking that all the Jews working on the other side of the Bug be returned to Tulcin. My appeal received no response, and today there is no one left to send back. My personal intervention on behalf of Mrs. Segall and Rosengarten in Tulcin was favorably received, but the men and their families were killed two days earlier with the rest. I get daily SOSs from very valuable people (survivors of the June, 1942, Cernauti deportations), but I cannot do much for them because the process is too slow. . . . The remaining 550 Jews in that district should be brought to Moghilev. . . . Make every effort and spare no expense to telegram an order to Tulcin. . . . We must act quickly because we think on March 1, they (the Germans) will ask for more workers to cross the Bug."

---

The Jagendorfs, Moses Katz and his family, and several other prominent Jews left Moghilev for Romania on March 7, 1944, one day after the orphans were repatriated and thirteen days before the Soviets recaptured the city.

Max Schmidt told me that Jagendorf did not bid farewell to the Turnatoria staff: "We were shocked and angered to discover that their leader had left them behind at a time of great danger." Schmidt describes the terror in Moghilev in early March, 1944, as the exiles awaited the retreating German Army:

"The stillness before the storm was unbearable. The Turnatoria, now under the direction of Engineer Popescu, remained in operation officially, but everyone thought only about what he would do when the inevitable will occur. One day we heard a rumor that German soldiers had opened their storehouses and were distributing food to the people. My wife found out that women actually were receiving sugar, flour, cooking oil, bread, and other items we had done without for a very long time. She joined the queue and watched soldiers simply let the people walk in and take whatever they wanted. Suddenly a very brutal German military police unit appeared and opened fire on the crowd. The soldiers returned the fire, and the people fled in panic. My trembling but uninjured wife could not tell me how many casualties resulted. We expected reprisals, but none came, probably because the Russian partisans were intensifying their attacks on the Germans and Romanians.

"Late one night in mid-March, 1944, a Russian military patrol, led by a young second-lieutenant, entered the Turnatoria housing unit. We welcomed the patrol with cheers, but our joy was dashed when the young officer accused the Jews of having dragged the Russians into the war to fight our battles against Hitler.

"The following day I walked to the town and saw a sickening sight: Ukrainian peasants blithely undressing the corpses of blood-soaked German and Romanian soldiers. That afternoon I spoke to a local Jew who worked in the Turnatoria. He told me that he had joined the partisans in order to take revenge on the Germans and Romanians for killing his entire family. He had already shot one soldier each for his mother, his father, his brothers, and sisters—a total of ten. He still had some reckoning to do with the local Ukrainians, but that would come later.

Dr. Meyer Teich, the most prominent Jew in the district following Jagendorf's departure, wrote about his final days in the Sargorod Lager:

"As the fleeing Germans spilled in from Uman, the town's [Romanian] authorities prepared to withdraw. On March 16, 1944, we remained alone in the town. German units passed by . . . accompanied by Hiwis (black-uniformed Ukrainian collaborators). A pogrom atmosphere descended upon the town. . . . Our people hid in hollows beneath cellars and in catacombs dating back to Turkish times. . . . These were the most fearful days we endured. . . .

"On the morning of March 20, 1944, a Russian cavalry unit entered Sargorod. I was summoned to a meeting with a general and partisan leaders to sign a declaration of the town's surrender. The general thanked me for the help we had given the resistance and the local population. . . . The following day was taken up with investigations of the ghetto period by Russian officers who were former professors at the Moscow University. They praised our Jewish committee.

"The following morning, these officers were replaced by security agents of the NKVD, heralding the era of disillusionment. They seized our supplies, leaving nothing for the needy. They confiscated the clothes we had received from Bucharest . . . and threatened to arrest me if I refused to surrender all the community property. When I would not hand over the ledgers, the cash, and other valuables, they threw me in jail. After four days of unbelievable intimidation, I relented and signed over the inventory of our fully-stocked pharmacy . . . and cash amounting to 600,000 lei ($3,000), a large sum in marks, and 100 rubles in gold.

". . . Then the security agents began to terrorize us with

searches, jailings, exile, conscription into the army, and forced labor. . . . The interventions of the partisan commander were of no avail. I was incarcerated in one of the dreaded prisons in Vinnitsa until they freed me in November, 1944, 'with apologies.' Five months later, I led 3,000 deportees back to Romania.

"In the district of Moghilev, about 70–80% of the deportees were saved and repatriated. . . . In the other districts (of Transnistria) only 20–30% returned. Some places had no survivors."

---

On March 10, 1944, ten days before the Soviets retook Moghilev, Marshal Antonescu consented to a general repatriation of the deportees. In the confusion, many deportees trailed the advancing Soviets across the Dniester, until the Soviets sealed the border. They regarded the deportees from northern Bukovina and Bessarabia (territories ceded to Stalin in June, 1940) as Soviet citizens. The border was reopened for a short period in April, 1945, allowing the return of some 7,000 Jewish exiles to Romania. Thousands remained behind, their fate unknown.

After arresting suspected collaborators and "bourgeoisie capitalists" among the deportees, the Soviets conscripted able-bodied men and women into military service and forced labor. According to Jacob Vogel, the Soviets drafted some 400 of the "liberated " Turnatoria workers into the Red Army. Most of them were killed or wounded when German warplanes strafed their train. The Soviets enslaved Jacob Vogel and nine other Bukovina deportees in the iron works factory, which under Soviet management, made hand grenades as well as tractor parts. Vogel finally escaped in 1955, after serving fourteen years in the Turnatoria at hard labor.

---

During the fall and winter of 1944–1945, accused war criminals were court-martialed. The following spring, under the pro-Soviet Petru-Groza regime, the People's Court took up the matter. Investigators experienced difficulty in obtaining documentary evidence and had to rely heavily on eye-witness testimony. Most Jewish survivors, still traumatized and disenfranchised, had no faith in

Romanian justice and refused to testify. They thought only of covering their nakedness, finding something to eat, and arranging passage to Palestine.

In May, 1945, the People's court prosecuted the governor of Bukovina and his aides, the commanders of the Vapniarca, and other war criminals who had operated in Bessarabia, Bukovina, and Transnistria. The many who had escaped were sentenced in absentia.

On April 13, 1945, the former prefect of Moghilev, Constantin Nasturas, wrote to the "Highly Esteemed Mr. Engineer Jagendorf" in Bucharest, requesting a letter of vindication. Nasturas emphasized the fact that, as prefect, he had to follow orders but did everything in his power to carry them out humanely. He drew a parallel to Jagendorf, who, as president of the committee and as "a good father fighting for a good cause" also had followed orders by "not fighting or resisting the measures which had to be applied." The former prefect then attested to his benevolence: ". . . I gave orders not to take excessive measures against the Jews. I overlooked the fact that Jews bought food in the public market after hours. I helped organize sanitation to improve the public health. I allowed enterprises and artisan shops, so that Jews could earn a living. . . . I postponed as long as possible the evacuations to Scazinet and closed the camp after a few months. . . ."

Jagendorf responded to Nasturas' request in a letter from Bucharest, dated May 31, 1946:

"As I prepare to leave Europe to engage in my profession after a Calvary of eight years, I regard it as an honorable duty to . . . express gratitude, in my name and in the name of the tens of thousands of Jewish deportees who lived in Moghilev. In your capacity as prefect . . . you acted humanely in carrying out the orders of your superiors. . . . You never added to our suffering . . . but tried your best to ameliorate our desperate situation, softening the orders you received. . . . You were removed from Moghilev to Tulcin as punishment for your humanity and understanding. . . ."

Jagendorf's forgiving response to Nasturas may have been influenced by the fact that Jewish leaders in Transnistria were not exempt from prosecution as war criminals. On July 2, 1945, the People's Court had found Mihail Danilof guilty of contributing to the nation's disaster, collaborating in the persecution of the deportees, and profiteering. He was sentenced to twenty-five years in prison, loss of civil rights for ten years, and confiscation of property.

On August 20, 1946, ten days before the Jagendorfs emigrated, Mihail Danilof filed an appeal in which he stated, "Regarding the accusation that I helped the Antonescu authorities to organize ghettos for the unfortunate people, the ghetto was organized by the prefect of Moghilev in compliance with an order of the governor of Transnistria. . . . Regarding the evacuations, I had no role. The evacuation orders were issued by the prefect of Moghilev, and the only one obligated to take all necessary measures to execute the evacuation was the president of the Jewish Committee, Engineer Jagendorf. . . ." Danilof's arguments were rejected by the court.

Anticipating possible vendettas after the war, Jagendorf armed himself with the files of the Jewish Committee, which he spirited out of Moghilev and, later, out of Romania. The People's Court, which relied on Jagendorf's testimony in a number of cases, did not indict the engineer. A secret Jewish panel, however, reportedly summoned Jagendorf to answer charges brought by survivors. Jagendorf engaged Jean Cohen as his attorney, but the case became moot when the Jagendorfs emigrated.

The brief trial of Ion Antonescu was not held until April 25, 1946, twenty months after he was overthrown in a palace coup. The former military dictator was found guilty and executed by firing squad. Also put to death were Mihai Antonescu, former president of the council of ministers; General Constantin Vasiliu, former undersecretary of police and security; and Gheorghe Alexianu former governor of Transnistria. Radu Lecca, former general commissar for Jewish questions, received a last-minute reprieve.

Dr. Teich recalls the evening he learned of the executions:

"One Saturday night in June, 1946, I was attending a Yehudi Menuhin concert in Bucharest. During intermission, an announcement came over the loudspeaker informing us that at 6:00 P.M., the sentences of General Ion Antonescu, Gheorghe Alexianu and the other major war criminals had been carried out. They were shot, the bodies burned, and the ashes scattered to the winds, denying their reactionary and anti-Semitic friends a pilgrimage site."

Historian Jean Ancel has called the trial and execution of Ion Antonescu "a propagandistic and educational failure." In the nearly two years between the time of Marshal Antonescu's arrest and his trial, the Romanian economy had been wrecked by the Soviets, who plundered the nation of its factories, machine tools, oil, grain, meat, and manufactured goods. The Kremlin demanded heavy war reparations as well. Romanians endured mistreatment at the hands of Soviet occupation forces, a bloody power struggle between the Communist Party and the two "traditional" (Liberal and Peasant) parties, and soaring inflation. In such an environment, the execution of Ion Antonescu struck the masses as an act of political expediency rather than one of justice. Dr. Ancel concludes that the war trials failed in the "re-education of the young generation, the defascization of the country . . . the suppression of anti-Semitic myths."

---

On December 23, 1946, Siegfried and Hilda Jagendorf arrived destitute in America, their suitcases filled with bundles of documents and memorabilia from Moghilev. Using the archives he had appropriated from the file drawers of the Jewish Committee in Moghilev, Jagendorf pressed his reparations claim against the Federal Republic of Germany, contending that the Nazis had a hand in the persecution and enslavement of Romanian Jews in the occupied Ukraine. In eventually winning his case, Jagendorf helped open the way for other Transnistria survivors to receive German restitution payments. The Romanians have never paid reparations.

In 1948, the Jagendorfs moved to southern California, where they joined Siegfried's sister Bertha, who had emigrated to America from Bukovia some forty years earlier. Bertha's daughter, Clara Coskey, helped her uncle get a job at the western division of the electrical contracting corporation, Fischbach & Moore. Hired as a project estimator, he soon was joined at F&M by Gus (Gustav) Sperling, son of Jagendorf's sister Betti. Sperling recalls:

"My uncle adjusted quite well to the American style of life, considering his stage of life. . . . In his new job, he had to learn all the little details of construction, which were considerably different from the German method. His co-workers were helpful and patient, and he became quite proficient. For three years prior to his retirement, he was chief estimator of the Los Angeles office."

Jagendorf established a personal relationship with his employer, Allen Fischbach, who one day revealed that he had been saved by a German officer from a lynch mob after having parachuted into enemy territory during an American bombing mission. Fischbach had wanted to reward his rescuer but did not know how to locate him. Jagendorf contacted the office of West German Chancellor Konrad Adenauer, which promptly supplied the name. Fischbach treated the man to a tour of the United States and invited Jagendorf to join them. He also bought the German a new automobile and awarded him a generous monthly stipend for life.

Jagendorf was soon elevated to department head. Milton Abbazia, his rival for the position, remembered his European co-worker:

"The level he started at was demeaning for him, but he made a decent adjustment. To boost his prestige, he was always talking about his studies at the University of Heidelberg and his contacts with famous people. At first, he got a lot of assistance from us. We thought he could be trusted, but the things we told him ended up in our employer's ear. He was a skilled double agent and a master at putting pressure on influential people."

Francis S. Kellstrom, general manager of the western division, told me that Jagendorf would discipline his six subordinates by placing his business card on their desks whenever they came to work more than five minutes late. "And it was very effective," said Kellstrom, approvingly, "it corrected their shabby work habits."

Gustav Jastrow, F&M's controller, recalled that Jagendorf demanded thoroughness, "all t's crossed and i's dotted, every estimate handed in on time. He was demanding but not abusive. He came across as a European, dressing formally and sporting a long cigarette holder. His wife, Hilda, gave my daughter lessons in Viennese cooking."

In his later years, Jagendorf often complained about not having received the credit he deserved for saving so many lives during the Holocaust. He accused his detractors of pettiness and jealousy. To defend his name and honor, Jagendorf began in 1956 to write his memoir, calling it, *JAGENDORF: My Story of World War II—The True Story of How 100,000 of My People Were Saved.*

After completing the manuscript, an effort that occupied him for more than a decade, Jagendorf reportedly traveled to Yad Vashem, the Holocaust Martyrs' and Heroes' Remembrance Authority in Jerusalem and offered to donate the Moghilev archives on condition that the institution publish his manuscript as written. When he was told that scholars would first have to study the contents, Jagendorf withdrew the offer.

On September 5, 1970, Siegfried "Sam" Jagendorf succumbed to cancer and heart disease at the Julene Convalescent Hospital in Sun City, California. His death certificate listed him as "chief engineer" at Fischbach & Moore. Three days later, in the presence of family members, he was eulogized by Ben Schwartz and Julius Lipnick, officials of Temple Beth Shalom in Sun City. His cremated remains were buried at the Perris Valley Cemetery in Riverside County, California. Upon Hilda Jagendorf's death, she was cremated (January 11, 1983) and laid to rest next to her husband.

---

Eighteen years after his death, I began researching the Siegfried Jagendorf story by interviewing his daughters, Elfreda Stern and Edith Gitman in Dayton, Ohio. I learned from them that Rifka and Arnold Auerbach of Paris were just then in New York to attend a wedding. In his memoir, Jagendorf described how he rescued Arnold from a firing squad after Rifka, a Turnatoria kitchen worker, asked him to intervene with the gendarme commander. I met the Auerbachs in Port Washington, Long Island. They confirmed the accuracy of the account but added that the engineer had behaved like a dictator, inspiring Romanian guards to salute him. I left my first meeting with Turnatoria survivors perplexed by their lack of gratitude and unwillingness to cooperate.

In the weeks that followed I located several other former Turnatoria workers, all male engineers who had been in their late teens or early twenties at the time of the exile. They justified Jagendorf's despotic behavior as a necessary response to the pervasive lawlessness in Moghilev and credited him with not only having saved their lives, but guiding their future careers.

Then, in February, 1989, I met Engineer Max Schmidt. At age 80, the former deputy technical superintendent of the Turnatoria looked frail, his wiry frame arched to one side. He spent his days and nights in his Manhattan apartment nursing his wife, Paula, who had been confined to bed for seven years following a stroke. The childless couple had been married for 55 years, having survived the deportations together. Mr. Schmidt opened his door to me, unlocking the mysteries of Moghilev. Certain recollections stirred him to tears. He frequently excused himself to comfort his wife in the adjoining room. So it continued until her death.

Schmidt's initial assessment of Jagendorf was positive but qualified. He spoke of a love–hate relationship, likening the Turnatoria director to a stern parent. Schmidt admired Jagendorf's courage in confronting the Romanians but could not forgive him for leaving Moghilev before the liberation.

In the summer of 1989, I traveled to Israel to complete my research and to interview a group of former Turnatoria workers who lived in a suburb of Haifa. On the night of the scheduled meeting, I was picked up by a talkative taxi driver wearing an old European-style cap over greying red hair.

"What brings you to Israel?" he asked.

"I'm working on a book about Transnistria. Ever hear of the place?"

"I was there," he replied.

"Actually, the book is on Moghilev–Podolski."

"That is exactly where I was."

"What is your name?" I asked.

"Yehiel Rosensweig."

"What did you do in Moghilev?"

"I was the horse-and-cart driver."

"Then you must know the name Engineer Jagendorf."

"Is he alive?"

"He died almost twenty years ago. What can you tell me about him?"

"If there is a *Gan Eden* (heaven)," he said, turning around to face me, "that is where you will find him."

# ACKNOWLEDGMENTS

First and foremost, it was the vision and determination of the late Siegfried Jagendorf that resulted in the publication of his memoir twenty-one years after his death and on the fiftieth anniversary of the mass deportations of Romanian Jews to Transnistria. Hilda Jagendorf, his wife, played a key role in preserving the supporting documentation by donating it to Yad Vashem, Jerusalem. The Jagendorfs' daughters Elfreda Stern and Dr. Edith Gitman and grandsons Lawrence J. Gitman and Ralph Stern are to be commended for recognizing the historical value of the unpublished memoir and for insisting on a truthful portrayal of it's author. I am grateful to them for giving me complete access to Siegfried Jagendorf's private papers and for providing the family photos that illumine this edition. I am also indebted to Siegfried's nephews Gustav Sperling and Adalbert Regenstreif, whose recollections and insights contributed greatly to my understanding of the author.

It has been my good fortune to work with HarperCollins' Carol Cohen, an editor of rare insight and integrity. In her soft spoken manner, she provided steadfast support and wise counsel.

A number of Transnistria survivors answered my appeal for eye–witness accounts and allowed me to tape their painful testimony. They deserve acknowledgment: Joseph Auslander (Paris), Joseph Biener (New York), Mark Brandman (New York), Edith Goodman (St. Paul), Berthold Gropper (Haifa), Jack Morgenstern (New York), Wolf Renner (Haifa), Fanny Rosen (San Diego), Yehiel Rosensweig (Haifa), Herman Sattinger (Brooklyn), David Scharf (Haifa), Michael Scherzer

(Haifa), Meir Shefi (Ramat Gan), Dr. Pepi Summer (Buffalo), Jacob Vogel (Cleveland), and Herta Wohll (Haifa). Special thanks to Max Schmidt of New York, whose formidable powers of recall, sharpness of mind, and fluency in languages, aided me immeasurably in reconstructing the Turnatoria story.

Author Ion C. Butnaru, my principal research consultant, deserves recognition for his outstanding job of immersing me in the sad history of Romanian Jewry. His annotated translations of hundreds of documents from the Jagendorf Archive at Yad Vashem constituted the basis of the chapter commentaries.

I also received the generous support of Dr. Jean Ancel, Romania specialist at Yad Vashem; Dr. Avigdor Shachan, author of a comprehensive book on Transnistria; Dr. Shmuel Ben-Zion, foremost authority on the orphans of Transnistria; Shraga Yeshurun, expert on the politics of the Moghilev Jewish Committee; and Dr. Sybil Milton and Dr. Radu Ioanid of the United States Holocaust Memorial Museum, Washington D.C. In the spirit of cooperation and a shared desire to retrieve Transnistria from historical obscurity, these scholars have freely offered me the fruits of their research, granted interviews, and commented on the accuracy of the work.

Several friends read the manuscript with an editor's eye, offering welcome suggestions that have enhanced the book. Many thanks to Charles Allen, Jr., Itzhak Artzi, Eric Blau, Martin Bressler, Judith Hirt-Manheimer, David Kellogg, Esther Kornecki, Rabbi Robert Orkand, Steven Schnur, and Joy Weinberg. I received additional translation help from Regina Bauer, Malka Herbstman, and Rabbi Bernard Zlotowitz.

This book would not have been possible without the resources of institutions devoted to Holocaust remembrance and research, most notably Yad Vashem, The Holocaust Martyrs' and Heroes' Remembrance Authority in Jerusalem. I also received assistance from the following institutions and organizations: Center for Holocaust Studies (Brooklyn), YIVO (New York), The Beate Klarsfeld Foundation (New York), United States Holocaust Memorial Museum (Washington, D.C.), Museum of the Jewish Heritage: A Living Memorial to the Holocaust (New York), Yale Video Archives for Holocaust Testimonies (New

ACKNOWLEDGMENTS

Haven), National Archives (Washington D.C.), Beth Hatefutsoth—Museum of the Jewish Diaspora (Ramat Aviv), Beit Lohamei Haghetaot, Ghetto Fighters House (Kibbutz Lohamei Haghetaot), and the Center for Research of Romanian Jewry, Hebrew University (Jerusalem).

# SOURCES

Ancel, Jean, (ed.) *Documents Concerning the Fate of Romanian Jewry during the Holocaust.* The Beate Klarsfeld Foundation. New York: 1986. A twelve-volume, 7,361-page compilation of reproduced documents selected by Dr. Ancel, Romania specialist at Yad Vashem in Jerusalem. Volume 5 concentrates on the Transnistria tragedy; Volume 12 provides English summaries of the documents, which are predominently in Romanian and German.

Ancel, Jean and Lavi, Theodor. Rumania, *Encyclopedia of Jewish Communities (Pinkas Hakehillot).* 2 vols. Jerusalem: 1969, 1980. Part of a series of memorial books documenting the fate of European Jewish communities in the Holocaust. In Hebrew.

Ancel, Jean. "The Romanian Way of Solving the 'Jewish Problem' in Bessarabia and Bukovina, June–July, 1941." Yad Vashem Studies, 19:187–232. Jerusalem, 1988. Examination of Romania's deliberate policy of genocide in these two provinces.

Bandot, Marcel et al (ed.) *The Historical Encyclopedia of World War II.* Facts On File, Inc. New York: 1980.

Ben-Zion, Shmuel. "Jewish Children in Transnistria during the Holocaust." Doctoral dissertation, University of Haifa, 1986. A thorough examination of the rescue efforts on behalf of the orphaned Romanian children beyond the Dniester River. In Hebrew.

Butnaru, Ion C. *The Forgotten Holocaust. (Holocaustul Uitat)* Tel Aviv: 1985. A pioneering work that examines the historical roots of the Romanian Holocaust. In Romanian.

Carp, Matatias. *The Black Book of Jewish Suffering in Romania, 1940–1944. (Cartea Neagra Suferintele Evreidor din Romania)* Vol. 3, Transnistria. Bucharest: 1947. A day-by-day chronology of the Romanian Holocaust. In Romanian.

Filderman (Wilhelm) Archive. Yad Vashem, Jerusalem. Includes original letters and reports related to the Transnistria exile. Mostly in Romanian and German.

Fischer, Julius S. *Transnistria: The Forgotten Cemetery.* New York: 1969. Survey of Transnistria.

Gilbert, Martin. *The Holocaust: A History of the Jews of Europe during the Second World War.* Holt, Rinehart, and Winston. New York: 1986.

Gilbert, Martin. *The Macmillan Atlas of the Holocaust.* Macmillan Publishing Co. Inc. New York: 1982.

Gold, Hugo. *The Story of the Jews in Bukovina. (Geschichte Der Juden In Der Bukowina)* Vol. 2. Olamenu. Tel Aviv: 1962. Description of the communities in Bukovina devastated during the Holocaust. In German.

Gutman, Israel. (ed.) *Encyclopedia of the Holocaust.* 4 vols. Macmillan Publishing Co. New York and London: 1990.

Hilberg, Raul. *The Destruction of the European Jews.* 3 vols. Holmes & Meier, New York and London: 1985.

Jagendorf (Siegfried) Archive. Yad Vashem, Jerusalem. Original documents from the files of the Moghilev Jewish Committee, 1941–1944. Mostly in Romanian and German.

Malaparte, Curzio. *Kaputt.* E. P. Dutton & Co., Inc. New York: 1946. Italian war correspondent's graphic descriptions of Romanian savagery against Jews during World War II.

Nagy-Talavera, Nicholas. *The Green Shirts and the Other: The History of Fascism in Hungary and Rumania.* Hoover Institution Press, Stanford University, Stanford: 1970.

Roth, Cecil. (ed.) *Encyclopedia Judaica.* 16 vols. Keter Publishing House Ltd. Jerusalem: 1972.

Safran, Alexandre. *Resisting the Storm, Romania 1940–1947: A Memoir.* Yad Vashem, Jerusalem: 1987. The exiled chief rabbi of Romania recounts his interventions on behalf of his embattled people.

Shachan, Avigdor. *Burning Ice: The Ghettoes of Transnistria (Bekfor Halohat: Ghetaot Transnistria).* Beit Lohamei Haghetaot. 1988. History of the Jewish exile in Transnistria, incorporating the author's memoir of survival. In Hebrew.

Schectman, Joseph B. "The Transnistria Reservation." YIVO Annual 13:178–196. New York, 1953. One of the first scholarly studies of Transnistria published in English.

St. John, Robert. *Foreign Correspondent.* Doubleday & Co. New York: 1957. Recollections of an American war correspondent in Romania.

Teich, Meyer. "The Self-Administration of Jews in the Sargorod Ghetto" In Studies of Heroism in the Holocaust Period. (ed.) Shaul Esch. Bialik Foundation, Yad Vashem, Jerusalem: 1959. One of the most prominent Jewish leaders in Transnistria recounts how his colony survived the perils of deportation. In Hebrew.

Yeshurun, Shraga. "The Self-Administration of the Bukovina Jews in the Moghilev Ghetto." Master's thesis, Haifa University, 1979. Examination of the Jewish Committee in Moghilev and Jagendorf's key role. In Hebrew.

# INDEX

Note: page numbers followed by a C refer to the Commentary.

*203*

Note: page numbers followed by a C refer to the Commentary.

Note: page numbers followed by a C refer to the Commentary.

Note: page numbers followed by a C refer to the Commentary.

Note: page numbers followed by a C refer to the Commentary.

Note: page numbers followed by a C refer to the Commentary.

Note: page numbers followed by a C refer to the Commentary.